In Search of
Theological Modesty

In Search of
Theological Modesty

Biblical Lessons

William Liss-Levinson

RESOURCE *Publications* · Eugene, Oregon

IN SEARCH OF THEOLOGICAL MODESTY
Biblical Lessons

Resource Publications
An Imprint of Wipf and Stock Publishers
199 W. 8th Ave., Suite 3
Eugene, OR 97401

www.wipfandstock.com

ISBN 13: 978-1-62564-823-5

Manufactured in the U.S.A.   04/28/2015

"... and my soul should be like dust to all,
open my heart into your Torah. .."

—Petitional prayer at the end of
the traditional *Amidah* prayer

"Only when we approach God in a state of humility
can we be open to learning the Torah"

—Attributed to the public discourses of
Rabbi Menachem Mendel Schneerson

CONTENTS

SECTION III—GOD CALLS AND OUR CALLING

SECTION IV—ON THE ROAD: THE DESERT JOURNALS

SECTION V—JOURNEYS: THE PROCESS IS THE PRODUCT

ACKNOWLEDGEMENTS

I AM EXTRAORDINARILY GRATEFUL to all the staff at Resource Publications, a division of *Wipf & Stock Publishers*. Your commitment to publishing books which you believe are of value, interest and importance in theology will enable the concept of theological modesty to have a wider audience.

Many of these chapters have appeared in earlier iterations over the past five years in the *GNS Scope*, a publication of the Great Neck Synagogue. Heartfelt thanks to Diane Rein, Editor and Andrew Allen, Artistic Director for the wonderful ways in which you have allowed me to share some of my thoughts in print. Rabbi Dale Polakoff of the Great Neck Synagogue, thank you for always being willing to engage with me in challenging conversations regarding interpretations of and struggles with the Torah's text. I am blessed with wonderful family and friends, whose love, friendship and support over the years sustain me; far too many to mention. I do want to acknowledge just a few people who have very specifically been a part of my theological struggles and development over the years as it relates to my writing this book: Benjy Gampel & Miriam Schacter, Carol Silk Hait, Harriet Sherman Schimel, Paul & Irene Marcus, Sharyn Falkenstein, Rabbi Meir Mitelman, Rabbi Brahm Weinberg, Rabbi Mordecai Waxman (of blessed memory), Eve Keller and Samuel Klein. You each have a special share in this work.

My parents, Aaron (of blessed memory) & Sylvia Levinson, made their own mid-life journey towards more traditional observance of Judaism. My father remarkably never suggested that his path was the right one, but felt strongly that some denominational affiliation and practice of Judaism was what was most essential. And to my mother, now ninety-four years old, you never cease to amaze me with your life-long sense of a very personal relationship with God. My in-laws, Morris & Gertrude Liss (of blessed memory), were models of the very best combination of strong Jewish identity, tolerance and acceptance of others, and a keen sense of social justice. Their legacy endures in their children, grandchildren and great-grandchildren.

To our dear children: Bluma & Jeff Sussman, Rivka Liss-Levinson & Ben Aronin, and our delightful grandchildren, Marc Aaron, Sadie Annaliss and Jordan Micah. You are blessings in my life and sources of immeasurable joy. You also represent the next generations of the Jewish people and understand that we all bear responsibility for making this world a better place.

Words cannot suffice to express my love for, and gratitude to, my wife, Nechama Liss-Levinson. Friends since we were fifteen and married now for forty-two years, your love, support, understanding, wisdom, kindness, patience and unwavering moral compass have been the major influence in my life. Our journeys together, virtual and metaphysical, are the rich tapestry of what has been, and the promise of, God-willing, the future that lies ahead for us. Who I am, and what I have been able to accomplish in life, including this book, is a tribute to the incredible gift of your being.

Creator of the Universe, I sometimes think we have always been involved in a theological *pas de deux*. You dance far better than I, and I often make the mistake of being so theologically immodest as to believe that it is I who should be "leading" in this dance and You who should be following. Completing this book, I feel fortunate to say the traditional *Shehecheyanu* blessing, "Blessed are You, God, our Lord, Ruler of the Universe, who has given us life, sustained us, and allowed us to reach this day."

December 14, 2014/23 Kislev 5775
Great Neck, New York

INTRODUCTION

IN MY FIRST YEAR of afternoon Hebrew School, I learned a popular Israeli melody to the opening lines of Psalm 133, "How good and pleasant it is, brothers dwelling together." Fifty-five year later, the chasm between that idealized expression of a time long-past, or perhaps a time that never-was, and the sad realities of a fragmented Jewish community, pain me. I am not simply pained emotionally; I am theologically disturbed and troubled. I worry about the impact of what I see, and what the implications are for my children, my grandchildren and future generations to come. I worry about my soul and the souls of other Jews who, in their fervor to hold true to their principles and beliefs, may leave little or no room for anyone else who has a different perspective. I am concerned that Buber's "I-Thou" concept of an intensive relationship between God and an individual has been transformed into a spiritual reality show with a limited cast of players competing for "Who Will Be God's Real Partner?" And I worry deeply at the increasing numbers of disaffected Jews, with few ties to our people and traditions, who may be saying "A curse on ALL your houses."

The purpose of this book is to offer some perspectives that may enable us to reconceptualize ourselves as thoughtful, spiritual Jews. Through analysis of Biblical texts in the five books of the Torah, I will illustrate three special themes I see within Judaism: placing God, and not ourselves, at the center of the universe;

understanding the boundaries and limitations we have as human beings; and recognizing the dangers inherent in the certainty that one's beliefs and perspectives are the only ones reflective of God's truth and will. This book will hopefully paint backdrops of possibilities for Jews, regardless of their particular beliefs, rituals, and practices, to be open to the potential validity and worthiness of the views and perspectives of others, a concept which I call "Theological Modesty."

This book is intended primarily to raise some questions and suggest some possible answers that require one to look through a different lens. I suspect that it will find the warmest reception among those who already have similar-minded views, an inclination to this perspective, and those who are seeking an approach that will enable them to feel more comfortable as thoughtful and practicing members of the Jewish community. If this can serve as a further source of encouragement and support for those readers, I will be satisfied. For those whose views are rather disparate from mine and nonetheless choose to read the book, I hope that I can contribute to their looking at their own strongly-held beliefs and perspectives through a different lens that enables them to even entertain new possibilities and perspectives. For this, I will be delighted.

Because the chapters are each relatively brief, the book is well-suited to be incorporated into synagogue adult education programs and in a variety of other educational forums, through which these issues can be explored. Finally, for theologically committed people of other faiths, I have hopefully presented the Jewish texts and other Jewish sources in a manner such that they too will find value in these chapters. Issues of pluralism and openness to differing views are certainly very much alive in other faiths as well. Intra and inter-religious understanding is a challenge we all share.

Where shall we begin this journey in search of Theological Modesty? The words of the first century rabbinic sage *Akavya ben Mahalalel* come to mind, when he suggested that we must all ask ourselves ". . . From whence we came, where are we going, and before whom we will be ultimately called for an accounting and a reckoning?" (*Mishna Avot*, 3:1) From whence we came? Let us go back to the beginning, perhaps even before the opening words of the Torah, "In the beginning God created . . ." (Gen 1:1).[1]

1. All translations of Hebrew texts are mine unless otherwise noted. Whenever possible I have sought to avoid using male pronouns in referring to God.

SECTION I

THE GENESIS IS IN GENESIS

1

GOD CONTRACTS HIS PRESENCE
WHAT IS OUR QUID PRO QUO?

THE OPENING OF THE Book of Genesis, starting with the first words of the first sentence, "In the beginning of God's creating of the heavens and the earth . . ." (Gen 1:1) are fertile ground for discussion of the origins of humanity and the universe as well the particularistic origins of the Jewish people. The medieval commentator Rashi[1] notes that the Torah begins with the creation of the world, rather than with the creation of the Jewish people which begins with the first commandment to them as a nation from God, "This month shall be to you . . ." (Exod 12:2), the commandment for the celebration of the Passover sacrifice and meal. Rashi indicates that this means that the Torah is not merely a book of laws for Jews. On a very basic level, this introduction to the beginnings of the world and humanity contained in the book of Genesis serves as a vehicle to teach us universal values about how we are to conduct ourselves as occupants of this universe. Among these values is a notion of creation and creativity, which challenges us to attempt to bring order, purpose and meaningfulness to the chaos that exists in the world, in our communities and within our own lives.

---

1. An acronym for Rabbi *Shlomo Yitzchaki*, French rabbinic scholar (1040–1105), and author of, arguably, the most important of classic rabbinic commentaries on the Torah.

One of the endearing aspects of religion, religious beliefs and theological discussions (or eternally frustrating aspect, depending upon whether you are sitting within the circle of faith or outside it) is the desire to try to understand God. Although by definition unanswerable, questions related to knowing God, understanding God and understanding God's intentions form much of the content of many religions' discussions. Many streams of thought and voices throughout the history of the Jewish people have pursued this topic with regard to God and the creation story. So perhaps there is something that we need to explore that even pre-dates "In the beginning of God's creating . . ." from which we may gain some insights.

For the Lurianic[2] Kabalistic[3] thinkers, one prominent question focused on what God needed to do prior to creation in order to allow anything other than God to exist. Built around the Kabalistic notion of God's hidden essence, the *Ein Sof*[4], that which is entirely unknown and unknowable, they conceptualized this Divine Essence of God as contracting itself in order to allow the universe and anything else that was or would be other-than-God to come into existence as independent realities. This process of contraction in Hebrew is called *tzimtzum*. A second notion deemed as essential to creation, to the creation of free will for humanity, and for the fulfillment of God's ultimate will in creation, was that humanity engage in *tikkun*, or repair of the broken aspects of the world, in order to become worthy partners with God.

If we are to be partners with God, fulfilling what many have termed *Imitatio Dei* (that the moral attributes and behaviors we should demonstrate reflect the ways in which we try to be imitative of God), then these lessons should start even before the words "In the beginning" with *tzimtzum*. So, in what ways should each of us contract our own presence in order to allow others to exist?

2. Followers of Rabbi Isaac Luria (1534–1572), one of the pre-eminent medieval mystics.

3. Used here in the broad sense to refer to areas of Jewish thought, philosophy and teachings related to esotericism and mysticism.

4. Literally, "there is no end or limit" or "that which is limitless."

Is there a special *tikkun* that this will achieve? And how will that enable us and others to ultimately be partners in achieving a God-like mission?

Perhaps it will help us if we understand God's act of *tzimtzum* itself as reflective of the attribute of *chessed*, loving-kindness, of the highest order. The term *chessed shel emet*, an act of loving kindness of truth, refers to doing a kindness for which we expect nothing back in return. The prime example is the care we show in preparing a dead person's body for burial, where we know the deceased cannot repay us. But the Lurianic Kabalistic notion of *tzimtzum* really has at its foundation a God who, while certainly not needing to have anything else exist, nonetheless allows for the possibility of endless others to come into existence. God gives us life as an act of grace, not predicated on us giving anything back in return, thereby performing a *chessed shel emet*. When we, as members of humanity, allow for the presence of others by creating the space for them to express their views, opinions and perspectives, we too are allowing for something very important other than ourselves to exist. And whether we agree with those views or not, we validate their essential worth and right to share a place in the universe of discussion. By doing so, by enabling a community of people with shared worth and value to co-exist even if they are different or differ, we repair the existential loneliness that is inevitable when we feel that our very essence is not validated by others. And finally, it is only in a community of mutual respect and value that differing views and perspectives can draw upon each other and give birth to a truly creative process, to new worlds and possibilities.

We now are in a position to revisit Rashi's question and answer it, albeit with a different answer than Rashi chose to give.[5] Why did the Torah not begin with Exodus and the first commandment given to the Jewish people as a nation? To teach us that that our very existence as a covenantally-commanded people must

5. Rashi's answer, to my understanding, is a theological and political one that focuses on the importance of the presented historical antecedents of the Jewish people's relationship to God as the source of authority for their right to occupy the land of Israel and to enjoy a unique relationship with God.

be contextually understood within God's larger gift to humanity by which anything and any one of us are even permitted to come into existence. Each of us as Jews, and each of us as members of humanity, is fundamentally bound together to be creative and to be partners in the larger creative project of repairing God's world. Each of us, therefore, has a responsibility to God, the world and to our fellow human beings. If *tzimtzum*, contraction of God's presence, is an attribute for us to emulate, then we must first acknowledge the inherent worth, value and holiness of the other who stands before us, whether literally or symbolically, prior to our saying anything about who we are or what we want, think or believe. And we can continue to emulate God's contraction by not allowing our ego to become so large that we leave no space for anyone other than ourselves.

2

A TREE GROWS IN EDEN

AFTER THE INITIAL CREATION of a human [Adam] by God, we are told:

> And God planted a garden in Eden at the east, and He
> set the human whom He had fashioned there. And God
> caused every tree that was pleasant to the sight and good
> for eating to grow from the ground, and the tree of life
> within the garden and the tree of knowledge, good and
> evil. (Gen 2:8-9)

A simple reading of this Hebrew text reveals that the tree is described as the "tree of knowledge, good and evil" and not a "tree of knowledge of good and evil," as is typically found in many English translations. The salient feature of the tree initially does not appear to be that it is related to some level of understanding about the distinctions between what is "good" and what is "evil." Rather, the tree's essence is something related to knowledge itself, *daat*, which is both good and evil. Later in verses 16–17, God specifically permits Adam to eat of all the trees, except from this tree of knowledge, because " . . .in the day you eat from it you will die." It appears that "consuming" some ultimate knowledge, while perhaps having aspects of "good' associated with it, is also simultaneously "evil" such that Adam can cause his own death.

This unusual tree is named [along with the Tree of Life] after the description of all the other trees God caused to grow in the garden, which are referred to as being ". . . pleasant to the sight and good for eating . . ." perhaps implying that this tree of knowledge [and for that matter, the tree of life] possessed neither of these qualities. It is therefore extraordinary that as the story ensues in Chapter 3, the snake manages to convince Eve to eat of the tree of knowledge. Surely there were sufficient other fruit-bearing trees in the Garden that were pleasant to the sight and good for eating for Eve to choose from for nourishment.

And what was the cogent, persuasive argument that the snake used? Countering Eve's assertion that God instructed her not to eat of this tree or even to touch it because if so she would die, the snake suggests (v. 4–5):

> You won't die. Because God knows that in the day you eat from it your eyes will be opened, and you'll be like God, knowing good and evil. (Gen 1:4–5)

It is this promise of being Godlike that remarkably transforms Eve, who now in verse 6 suddenly sees that " . . .the tree was good for eating and that it was an attraction to the eyes, and the tree was desirable to bring about understanding . . ." Violating God's prohibition, Eve partakes herself and subsequently gives some of the fruit to Adam, who also eats, whereupon they both become newly aware of their pre-existing nakedness. Confronted by God, each player in the story "passes the buck" so to speak regarding responsibility for their actions. God curses all of them and Adam and Eve are cast out of the garden, with painful childbirth and toil in order to sustain a livelihood the curses on all humanity for the future. Why does God feel it necessary to cast them out?

> And God said, 'Here, the human has become like one of us, to know good and evil. And now in case he'll put out his hand and take from the tree of life as well, and eat and live forever. (Gen 3:22)

So what do we make of all this? God simply prohibited eating from the tree and indicated that failure to heed this would result in death, but gave no reason for the prohibition. God never instructed Adam not to touch the tree of knowledge, but Eve extends the prohibition to that as well. And why would Adam and Eve violate the one apparent restriction placed on them in Eden and risk what was supposed to be a certain resultant death? How is "to know good and evil" equivalent to becoming "like one of us?" God promised that Adam and Eve would die if they eat from the tree, yet instead imposes banishment from Eden. And why must they be banished? Because once having committed the sin of eating from the tree of knowledge, there is fear that the humans will now eat from the tree of life (something that God had never even prohibited Adam from doing) and thus live forever. A confusing picture at best.

Several possibilities emerge. The temptation to possess a God-like ability can create an overwhelming urge within us. It may distort our perception and judgments, propelling us to believe that we can know God, know God's motives, and therefore know some truth even beyond God. Hence, a snake can easily convince Eve of God's "real" intent. And the temptation can be so overwhelming that we can be in a danger zone simply by going down this path or reaching out in this direction. Adam and Eve did in effect die though their sin, in that they killed off a certain idyllic potential and forever created a more nuanced and complex life for all humanity to come. This new archetype of human being, however, offers other potentials, most notably creativity, which is symbolized by both the birth and work processes whereby we can realize the fruits of our own labors. So banishment from Eden is more than simply a reprieve from death; it is actually a new chance to live in the world productively.

And we dare not forget the blessing of being aware of our nakedness, which is also forever a by-product of the Eden experience. Each of us now has the ability to see each other and ourselves with clearer eyes. We can, as a result, be strongly attracted to each other or strongly repelled. We have the potential to see our own vulnerabilities, weaknesses and foibles, as well as those of others. And we can be aware and perhaps even "embarrassed" by who and what we are or have become, not necessarily in some neurotic way but in a manner that reflects personal insight and an awareness of ourselves within the context of our social relationships with others. Perhaps this too is a very good outcome!

3

SIBLING RIVALRY TO THE REFRAIN OF "NEARER MY GOD TO THEE"

THE TORAH, NEVER SHYING away from our flawed beginnings, wastes no time in going from the creation of the world and the sin of Adam and Eve to an epic story of sibling rivalry and fratricide. Adam and Eve bear two sons, first Cain and then Abel. Cain was a farmer and Abel was a shepherd. What compelled Cain to bring an ". . . offering to God from the fruit of the ground" (Gen 4:3) is certainly not clear, but his younger brother proceeds to copy this behavior.

> Abel brought, as well, from the firstborn of his flock and their fat. And God paid attention to Abel and his offering and did not pay attention to Cain and his offering. And Cain was very upset and his face was fallen. (Gen 4:45)

God asks Cain why he is upset, suggesting that he might want to somehow look inward and see what he could do to improve his situation, improve his offering or perhaps improve himself. Cain has no reply to God. Biblical scholar Richard Elliot Friedman[1] points out in his commentary on the Torah that in cases of sibling rivalry, the mere existence of the intruding younger sibling is often

---

1. Friedman, *Commentary on the Torah*, 27. (note to Gen 4:8)

experienced as an insufferable wound. Perhaps that's why no clear explanation is stated for Cain's upset. It wasn't that Abel copied his brother's initiative and wound up seemingly finding greater favor in God's eyes. The more fundamental problem, exemplified by this situation, was that the world, as minimally populated as it was at this point, wasn't "big enough" to contain both Cain and his brother Abel.

So what does Cain do? Oddly enough, the Torah recounts what appears to be a fragment ". . . and Cain said to Abel his brother" (Gen 4:8), without telling us what was the nature of this conversation. Various rabbinic legends offer fascinating versions of a dialogue between the two brothers, and Friedman tells us that contrary to the traditional Hebrew text, the Samaritan, Greek and Latin versions read " . . .and Cain said to Abel, 'Let's go into the field.'"[2] But perhaps the traditional text, in which Abel does not even reply to or in any other way seem to acknowledge Cain's conversational overture, can inform our subsequent analysis of this entire humanity-changing sibling interaction.

So what does occur? While in the field with Abel, Cain rises up against his brother Abel and kills him. There is perhaps no more direct response we can summon to the pain caused to us by someone whom we despise by virtue of their mere existence than by seeking to end his or her existence. And when God calls out to Cain, affording him the opportunity for some type of admission of guilt and perhaps contrition, Cain creates the first football strategy, otherwise known as the best defense is a good offense, i.e. "And he said, I don't know. Am I my brother's watchman?" (Gen 4:9). The first part is denial; simple, bold-faced denial of any knowledge or association with the act. The second part is denial of having any responsibility for the detested other. Friedman[3] makes a point of translating the Hebrew *shomer* as "watchman" as opposed to the classic [my brother's] keeper. Citing several other subsequent Biblical uses of the term *shomer,* he emphasizes how this term eventually is also used to convey loyalty to God. In effect, Cain says to

2. Ibid, 26 (note to Gen 4:8)
3. Ibid, 28 (note to Gen 4:9)

God in a somewhat perverse way, "My loyalty is to you God but not to my brother, my fellow human being."

The denouement continues in a famed conversation between God and Cain.

> And He [God] said: What have you done? The sound! Your brother's blood is crying to me from the ground! And now you're cursed from the ground that opened its mouth to take your brother's blood from your hand. When you work the ground it won't continue to give its potency to you. You'll be a roamer and rover in the earth. (Gen 4:10–12)

It is remarkable that in these three sentences where God holds Cain accountable for his actions there is such an emphasis on the "ground," in Hebrew *adama*. As we know, Cain's father, the first human created, was called Adam because he was formed from the dust of the ground. But is there another message that we can see here in God's words to Cain? Was this sin simply [sic] that he has introduced fratricide, and the act of murder in general, to the world, or is there something else that Cain has also done? Is God holding Cain accountable for having perpetrated something on Adam, symbolic of the essence of all humanity? The *adama*, the ground, serves as a symbol of the very foundations of our being. Cain, by killing his despised other and thus believing he could eliminate his competition, has tainted and forever diminished his own foundation and all of those to follow. He is as much a victim of his own crime as he is the perpetrator of the crime, a crime not only against his brother, but against all of humanity to come.

Cain, now acknowledging the depth of his guilt and awareness of the far-reaching implications of his action, says:

> And Cain said to God: My crime is greater than I can bear. Here you've expelled me from the face of the ground today, and I'll be hidden from your presence and I'll be a roamer and a rover in the earth and anyone who finds me will kill me. (Gen 4:13–14)

Cain now knows that the ground, upon which he had assumed he could always securely plant his feet, would now forever reject him. And whatever his relationship with God was, it would no longer be the same. Furthermore, by attacking and murdering his brother, Cain realized he had declared "Open Hunting Season" to the world and he himself was now the most likely target.

So what does God do in response to Cain's fears?

> And God said to him: Therefore anyone who kills Cain, he shall be avenged sevenfold. And God set a sign for Cain so that anyone who would find him would not strike him (Gen 4:15)

There is an interesting variation between the beginning of the sentence which references killing Cain, versus the symbol from God that is given to signal to others that they may not even strike Cain. The sign appears to be as much about protecting the rest of humanity from going down the same path that Cain took as it is about protecting Cain from being further harmed, beyond his own already self-inflicted wounds, by others.

What can we learn from this entire tale? In Cain's bold-faced, multi-level denial to God, we easily see the roots of a seemingly eternal human approach to coping with our inexcusable behavior toward a fellow human being. First, deny any knowledge of the behavior, then claim not to have any responsibility for the despised other. It is an approach, remarkably transparent, which still is widely utilized by individuals and nations alike. Next, we see that as human beings we have an amazing ability to convince ourselves that our alleged loyalty to God is so encompassing that it permits us to commit crimes against others, while believing that we are acting justly and in accordance with God's wishes. That argument in the extreme has served for centuries and into the present as the basis for horrors, atrocities and countless millions of lives lost, all backed by a pledge of loyalty to God. We also can see that an act seemingly against one despised other is actually an act against many others, as well as an act against one's self and against God. The despiser of the other is also easily transformed into the despised by every other, rejected by all and thereby distancing him/herself from God's presence.

Lastly, perhaps the mark of Cain is one that all of us should wear. It may be a universal gift that God gave to humanity that is intended to protect ourselves from ourselves; to resist our tendencies to want to strike, demolish or eradicate the other we don't like, don't understand, don't love, or simply wish didn't crowd our world and worldview through their mere existence. And inherent in this mark of Cain we should not forget that there may be a potential role that all of us can play in dealing with someone whom we know disagrees with and even despises us. Do we act like Abel and not even acknowledge that other person, perhaps intimating that we needn't hear their view, their pain, their anger, and thus in some way deny their very essence? As is the case with many symbols, the challenge to us is to understand and integrate their message into our daily lives. We too may need to create external reminders to help us be mindful to respect others.

4

THE RISE AND FALL OF
A TOWER IN BABEL

GENERATIONS COME AND GO. God destroys most of the world via a flood but spares Noah, his family and groups of the animal species in order to give us all a chance to start again and correct the human-created corruption and violence that permeated the world pre-flood. So what could be better to demonstrate that we learned our lesson than a group construction project? With a common mission and vision, and the shared challenges of a defined goal, it should have been a formula for success.

As Chapter 11 of Genesis opens, we are lulled into a false sense of optimism:

> And it was that all the earth was one language and the same words. And it was that when they were traveling from the east; and they found a valley in the land of Shinar and they lived there. And they said one to another: Come, let's make bricks and fire them. And they had brick for stone and they had bitumen for mortar. And they said, Come let us build ourselves a city and a tower ... (Gen 11:1–4)

There appears to be unity of understanding through a common language. Off on a common journey, these people find a common place and make a peaceful group decision to settle there.

Recognizing the natural resources available to them, they agree to work on a common project, making bricks. Apparently, although not explicitly stated, this was successful, for they then decide on a common creative use for these bricks, building a city and a tower. But something happens in their mission and vision, such that once again God is worried about the future of humanity—and it appears to be focused on the tower:

> And they said: Come on let's build ourselves a city and a tower and its top will be in the skies, and we'll make ourselves a name or else we'll scatter over the face of all the earth. (Gen 11:4)

Friedman[1] comments that this story is at its very core ambiguous. We are not told what the intention was of the people in building the tower whose top would be in the sky/heavens. And it is certainly not clear what their concern was regarding being scattered over the "face of the earth" unless their tower could reach up into the heavens.

Inherent in the brief description in verses 1–4 we see an ability to live with one another in a state of permanency, rootedness and cooperation, and a desire to bring themselves and thus all humanity once again closer to God through a shared vision, mission and goal. Was it the intent of these people to pursue what they believed were God's goals for humanity?

And yet, the ensuing passages describe God as seeing the building as an act of rebellion. Consistent with Adam and Eve, Cain and Abel, and the generation destroyed in the flood, humanity once again is in conflict with God:

> And God went down to see the city and the tower that the children of humankind [Hebrew: Adam] had built. And God said, Here they're one people and they all have one language, and this is what they've begun to do. And now nothing that they'll scheme to do will be limited. Come, let's go down and babble their language so that one won't understand another's language. And God

---

1. Ibid, p .46 (note to Gen 11:4).

scattered them from over the face of all the earth and
they stopped building the city. (Gen 11:5–8)

At first blush this is puzzling and troubling. In a modern
family drama, this would be akin to a critical father who walks in
on his children playing together peacefully and decides that they
now have the ability to scheme against him through their unity. So
he knocks down their blocks, sends them to their rooms spread
out across the house, and cuts the telephone lines so they can't
even communicate.

Perhaps the problem in this story begins with the desire for
the tower to reach into the skies/heavens and the concomitant wish
to make for themselves a "name." Maybe it even begins long before
that. Until God enters into the scene, already disturbed by what
is transpiring, God is not a character in the story of these people.
After traveling together and finding a suitable place to dwell, rich
with resources that feed their creative technological skills, these
people don't even offer the sacrifice of Cain, or Noah's post-flood
altar and sacrifice. This is humanity at its arrogant best, a nameless
people until God refers to them in verse 5 as the "children of Adam."
This may imply that they thought they had found and created their
own new Eden without needing God. Possessing the ability to
create bricks, they nonetheless pass on the opportunity to make
an altar, create a monument or in some other way mark the place
via an acknowledgement of God's place and role in their world.
Their desire to build a city seems to be consistent with humanity's
primary need for shelter. But this city's distinguishing feature is to
be a tower whose purpose does not seem to be to create a vantage
point from which to view visitors or to serve some primary need
for self-protection. This tower's sole purpose was to reach into the
very sky/heavens. Even here they fail to mention God's name, and
their articulated desire has nothing to do with wanting to be more
connected to God. Their arrogance is not about their technological skills, but rather is reflected in not knowing the limits of one's
space and place in the world. What is their purpose in reaching
to the heavens? It is to make a name for themselves lest they be
scattered over the face of the earth. Since the preceding chapters

of the Torah would indicate that individual names were given to people, apparently by their parents, we can assume that these people all had individual names too. So they were seeking some distinctive name for themselves as a group, something that would be so clearly defining that would enable them to recognize each other and be recognized by others even if they were eventually to be scattered across the earth. Sort of akin to "There goes one of the so-and-so's; you know, the ones who are right up there with God."

Destroying the people's ability to communicate through the creation of many languages can be seen in light of the opening lines to the entire story, where it is described that " . . .all the earth was one language and the same words." A world in which all were of one voice and one mind should not be confused with a world of unity of vision. Such unity is achieved through cooperation with others who may not be like you or share your views. Instead, by placing themselves at the center of a creative universe and excluding God, these people were perhaps even confounding themselves with God as they sought to create a space for themselves within the sky/heavens.

God's solution to this arrogance is indeed harsh and still plagues us today. A radical and far-reaching solution is imposed that will forever require us to struggle to know the other, to learn how to cooperate and compromise if we are to be understood and understand the other. We cannot all be of one voice, one word, and one mind. The creation of a common name and a shared identity does not define who and what we are for all times, for all peoples and for all purposes. We dare not delude ourselves by confusing our potential for soaring visions and seemingly boundless creativity as being indicative that we ourselves are God. When we look at the other, at one another, the different-than-us-other, even the despised other, the essential quality that we should see is that all of humanity is created *b'tzelem elohim*, in the image of God. And that recognition of the divine image is what should serve as a reminder that we are all of this earth, with enormous potential but also possessing inherent limitations. We are not the owners of a world, into which we invite God to be our guest; rather, WE are guests of God in this world.

5

JACOB: THREE CHANCES AND HE STILL DOESN'T QUITE GET IT RIGHT

JACOB, THE THIRD OF our Patriarchs (Abraham and Isaac being the first two) had two experiences of the divine in Genesis that perhaps forever set the stage for us as his descendants. In the first extraordinary encounter, Jacob, fleeing from his brother from whom he stole the rights of the first-born, sets forth on a journey to Haran to locate Laban his uncle. Stopping for the night, he has his famed dream (Gen 28:12–19) of a ladder, standing fixed on the ground yet with its top touching up to the heavens. On this ladder, Jacob sees angels of God, ascending and descending, and then God stands before Jacob and speaks to him as the God of his fathers Abraham and Isaac. Upon awakening, Jacob utters his famous words, "Surely God is in this place and I, I did not know."

In the classic Kotzker Chassidic[1] school of thinking, Jacob's problem was that his own "I," his own ego, was so dominant that it impeded his ability to be aware of God. The choice of the ladder may have been particularly important as a symbol that Jacob might well have missed too. As a vehicle for climbing, a ladder requires two things of us, both of which are necessary to ascend. We have

1. Followers of Menachem Mendel Morgensztern of Kotzk (1787–1859), better known as the Kotzker Rebbe, who was a Chassidic rabbi and leader.

to step up and we have to pull ourselves simultaneously. If we are passive, as opposed to actively seeking a new experience, we may well never take that first step, or subsequent steps, necessary to see what new heights we can reach. But that alone is insufficient. We must also simultaneously stretch, reaching towards the unknown, if we are to achieve new heights.

But rather than learning from his new-found awareness of his inability to sense God's presence on an immediate basis, Jacob names the place *Bet-El*, the house of God. The act of naming something is one which is laden with issues of precision, definition, proscription, domination and control. Jacob, in his haste and theological arrogance, further demonstrates his failure to realize what the Kotzker Rebbe so aptly stated, "Where do you find God? Wherever you let Him in."[2] Jacob still doesn't understand that in order to be open to God's presence, we must find an internal spiritual place within, rather than situating God solely in an external physical space. In addition, Jacob makes the place of his dream the "house of God," thereby excluding other individuals who may also have a sense of a personal relationship with God.

Later on, Jacob has a mystical experience on the eve of encountering his brother Esau. At night he is confronted by a man with whom he wrestles throughout the night. Rabbinic commentators have differing views as to whether this man is actually a "good angel" or in some way an evil-inclined angel, but all agree that he is indeed an angelic presence. In the morning, in exchange for letting his opponent go, Jacob exacts a blessing from this man/angel/divine spirit, including the new name Israel, because, as the angel says " . . .You have striven with God and men and *vatuchal*." (Gen 32:29). Many classical and modern commentators translate this last word as "and you have won out." I much prefer the translation noted by Friedman, "and you were able,"[3] which is grounded in the precise root and verb form of the Hebrew word *vatuchal*.

2. While most commonly attributed to the Kotzker Rebbe, it should be noted that it is also at times attributed to other prominent Chassidic masters of the same era.

3. Ibid, 112.

And of no lesser importance, "and you were able" seems more appropriate, for who among us could possibly strive with God and "win?" Jacob finished the race, so to speak; no small task on the one hand, but no records were made and certainly no wins.

Twice in this narrative, Jacob seeks to know the angel's name, perhaps another attempt by Jacob to control the other by knowing his name. Despite being rebuffed yet again, rather than learning from this, Jacob seeks further control through an act of naming and responds with theological arrogance. He names the place of his encounter *Piniel*, saying "I have seen God face to face." (verse 31). Here Jacob has overstated the nature of his interaction with, and experience of, God. And as a result of this experience, Jacob is wounded in his thigh, which must have left him permanently impaired in his ability to walk and perhaps, as a subtle message from God, a warning to be less theologically sure-footed in the future.

Jacob has a third missed opportunity to apply his understanding of God and God's role in the universe. This third occasion is rather different from the previous two episodes, and reflects both what he misses personally and how he also then failed to transmit a deeper sense of God to his own son Joseph. In Gen 37:4, we read of how Jacob favors Joseph and gives him a coat of many colors, indicative to his brothers that " . . .their father loved him the most of all his brothers." Joseph has two dreams, which further stir the pot of resentment. Perhaps in his adolescent foolishness, and certainly reflective of his thinly veiled hostility toward his brothers who despised him, Joseph feels compelled to tell his brothers the first of the two dreams. In this dream, Joseph recounts that they all are binding sheaves of wheat together in the field and the brothers' sheaves surround and bow down to his sheaf. The brothers, aptly but perhaps superficially, interpret this as Joseph's unconscious desire to dominate and rule over them, and they become even more despising of him. When Joseph has a second dream, not having learned anything from his previous experience, Joseph again feels compelled to relate the dream to his brothers, and now also relates it to his father Jacob. In this dream, Joseph envisions the sun and the moon and eleven stars bowing down to him. Jacob is angered by this and says:

> . . .What is this dream that you've had? Shall we come, I and your mother and your brothers, to bow to you to the ground? (Gen 37:10)

Joseph's brothers are jealous of him, but we are told in verse 11 " . . . and his father took note of the thing."

Jacob's interpretation in verse 10 is not dissimilar from his sons' interpretation of the first dream. It is apt, but incredibly limited. We see that Joseph's problem of arrogance goes far beyond issues of family dynamics and sibling rivalry. Jacob's failure to realize and show concern about this problem directly and immediately to his son Joseph reflects Jacob's third missed opportunity. Contrasting the first dream with the second, in the first Joseph at least has some semblance of equality of imagery in that he, like his bothers, is represented by his sheaf, and their sheaves bow to his sheaf. While a message of dominance and triumphalism, there is at least a modicum of pretense that they are of the same type or form. In the second dream, the very sun, moon and the stars, certainly symbolic to the patriarchs and matriarchs of God's overarching presence in the universe, bow to Joseph, the human being. Yes, it is an affront to what should be a more respectful attitude vis a vis his parents. But that is all that Jacob addresses in his anger to Joseph. Where is a statement that Joseph's dream also reflects arrogance by placing himself at the center of the universe? Why doesn't Joseph's dream evoke for Jacob his own earlier-learned lessons regarding the consequences of missing God's presence? Jacob had a theological responsibility as a parent, and perhaps a rare natural teaching moment, to deal with Joseph's delusions of grandeur that blurred the distinction between God and human beings. Jacob's "I" still obstructs his theological vision.

6

JOSEPH: SO FUNCTIONAL, YET SO FORGETTABLE

JOSEPH'S BROTHERS' INTENSE HATRED and jealousy eventually boil over and they contemplate murdering him in the later half of Chapter 37 of Genesis. The eldest brother Reuben intervenes and the brothers seize Joseph and cast him into a pit to decide his fate. Judah, the fourth of Jacob's sons, suggests that they sell him to the Ishmaelites. But in the midst of their deliberating, a band of Midianites comes along and removes Joseph and sells him to the Ishmaelites, who in turn bring him to Egypt. Joseph is then sold as a slave to Potiphar, chief of the guards and a key official to the Pharaoh. Joseph, because of what appears to be God's interventions, is highly successful in Potiphar's house and demonstrates abilities such that he is given overall responsibility for the management of Potiphar's household. A series of encounters with Potiphar's wife, who is sexually attracted to the very handsome Joseph, results in a false accusation of attempted rape, and Joseph is cast into prison. There God intervenes once again so that Joseph is seen in a favorable light by the Warden and is treated with kindness within the prison. He befriends two other prisoners who were Pharaoh's personal servants, the Royal Baker and the Royal Drink-Steward. Eventually each has a dream and presents the dreams to Joseph, who does say that he can interpret them but clearly acknowledges that understanding dreams is a skill in some way connected to God. Joseph interprets the dreams to the two, predicting death for the Baker but freedom and restoration to a position of power for the Drink-Steward. Of the latter, he requests that the Drink-Steward remember him and see that Joseph is released from prison. Joseph's interpretations are correct and the Baker is killed and the Drink-Steward is restored. However, "And the drink-steward did not remember Joseph. And he forgot him." (Gen 39:23)

How could the Drink-Steward have forgotten Joseph? Joseph should have been an important figure to him even prior to the successful interpretation of the dream, because the Warden had put Joseph in charge of all the prisoners. In addition, Joseph had specifically made the request to be remembered. Eventually, in the closing chapters of Genesis, Joseph is redeemed from prison after a delayed recollection by the Drink-Steward, and eventually successfully interprets Pharaoh's dreams. Explaining economic policy to Pharaoh, Joseph is put in charge of the land of Egypt and helps them through the crisis. Joseph is second only to Pharaoh and, as the book of Genesis draws to a close with Joseph's death, we learn that he is mourned by all of Egypt as if he were a Pharaoh.

Now fast forward to the opening of the book of Exodus:

> And a new king rose over Egypt who did not know Joseph. (Exod 1:8)

Rashi offers two classic theories about this. The first is that this was actually a new Pharaoh, and the second is that it was the very same Pharaoh of Genesis Ch.39, but he had developed new policies and attitudes. But how could a new Pharaoh, much less if it was the same Pharaoh, ever forget Joseph and all that he had done to save the land of Egypt and the Egyptian people? Perhaps more importantly, how did Joseph manage to be so functional and yet so forgettable on these two critical occasions?

Let's explore these questions through the lens of analyzing the qualities of relationships that endure versus those that appear to be strong but don't endure. It may be useful to think in terms of relationships that are built upon the premise of what someone functionally does for someone else (be it unilateral or reciprocal) versus relationships that are built upon a deeper quality of emotional value or connectedness. Joseph was clearly the brilliant Hebrew, whose talents were recognized and utilized, be it in positions of power and management in Potiphar's house, in the prison, or in his capacity as Pharaoh's senior advisor. God's direct interventions in the first two instances, as described in the Torah, may have given Joseph a competitive edge for his natural talents and abilities to surface and be recognized, and for others to benefit from them. But we don't really have a sense of what Joseph meant to any of these people beyond what smart solutions or ideas he brought to them. Fundamentally, he was respected as long as, and because, he was able to "deliver the goods." However, we have no sense of the relationship between Joseph and Pharaoh other than this functional one. Even with Joseph's death and the mourning by all of Egypt, one could imagine that Pharaoh and the Egyptian people surely grieved the functional loss of his talents.

So what message do we derive from this as it relates to our theme of theological modesty? It is not coincidental that Joseph, the arrogant adolescent with delusions of grandeur and a marked insensitivity to the feelings of his brothers and his parents, is someone who has problems in developing and sustaining enduring relationships. In both the abovementioned instances of being forgotten, Joseph's essence as a man of inherent value to the other (be it the Drink-Steward, Pharaoh or the Egyptian people) is nowhere to be found. Was it because he himself saw people as means to an end, in the first instance his freedom from prison and, in the second, his ascension to power and the ability to have dominion not only over the Egyptian people but over his family as well? Does Joseph's "I" obstruct his ability to see the value in others, ultimately subjecting him to the very same fate in his death? What does this say for us when we explore our relationships with people, and in particular, people who are different from us? Do we routinely develop relationships that are ones of convenience and functionality but are lacking an underlying respect and regard for the value of the other? Are there larger implications for alliances that form within Jewish communities, big and small, in which functional needs bring people together for a common cause or good, but the deeper value and respect for each other's very essence is never part of the equation? What are the global implications of these types of relationships?

Much to reflect upon as we move from Egypt into the desert, enroute to a small mountain called Sinai.

SECTION II

ON A SMALL MOUNTAIN IN A DESERT

7

". . . AND THE BUSH WAS NOT CONSUMED"

IF THERE IS ANY way in which I truly feel like I am standing at Mount Sinai receiving the Torah for the first time, it is when I read something that I have read for perhaps fifty years and am convinced that NEVER before have I seen those words. As the Torah reader this year read the opening chapters of Exodus, describing Moses' encounter with the burning bush, such a revelatory experience occurred for me.

> Moses was pasturing the flocks of Jethro, his father in law, the chief of Midian, and he led the flocks after the free pastureland, and he came to the mountain of God, to Horeb. An angel of the Lord appeared to him in a flame of fire from within the thorn bush, and behold, the thorn bush was burning with fire, but the thorn bush was not being consumed. So Moses said, Let me turn now and see this great sight, why does the thorn bush not burn up? The Lord saw that he had turned to see, and God called to him from within the thorn bush, and He said, Moses, Moses! And he said, here I am! And He said, "Do not draw near here. Take your shoes off your feet, because the place upon which you stand is holy soil." (Exod 3:1–5)

A close reading of the Hebrew text led to me to see several critical issues. The bush is *boer ba'eysh*, "burning in the fire," yet the bush is not *ukal,* "consumed." This is the description of the actual reality of that which was confronting Moses. But what is it that Moses experiences, as reflected in his statement in verse 3? The above-cited English translation of the text, a common one which I intentionally chose, states " . . .why does the thorn bush not burn up." Other translations go a step further and say " . . .is not consumed." Yet the critical word in Moses' statement of what he sees is *lo yivar,* which I feel more precisely means "will not burn." In effect, Moses specifically turns to look and sees something he knows is an unnatural event. Despite somehow having some sense of a fire, he cannot even see that the bush is burning! It is at this point that God, and not the angel of God referenced in the second verse as appearing in a flame of fire from within the bush, is now compelled to call out to Moses. We must ask ourselves: Why did Moses have such difficulty seeing that which was before him? Why was the angel of God, the intended God-presence of the experience, inadequate to the task? What was the purpose of this miraculous occurrence for Moses?

In order to proceed, we need to look at what we know of Moses from the preceding chapters. After he is saved from the basket in the Nile by Pharaoh's daughter, given the name Moses and taken to be raised as her son, we know nothing more from the text itself about what occurs in his infancy, toddlerhood, childhood or adolescence. Then we are told:

> Now it came to pass in those days that Moses grew up and went out to his brothers and looked at their burdens, and he saw an Egyptian man striking a Hebrew man of his brothers. He turned this way and that way, and he saw that there was no man; so he struck the Egyptian and hid him in the sand. He went out on the second day, and behold, two Hebrew men were quarreling, and he said to the wicked one, Why are you going to strike your friend? And he retorted, Who made you a man, a prince, and a judge over us? Do you plan to slay me as you have slain the Egyptian? Moses became frightened and said, Indeed, the matter has become known! Pharaoh heard of this incident, and he sought to slay Moses; so Moses fled

from before Pharaoh. He stayed in the land of Midian, and he sat down by a well. (Exod 2:11–18)

Whatever has inspired Moses, now an adult, he leaves the security of the royal palace and has a profound experience, one in which he clearly identifies with the oppressed Hebrews, his "brothers," and is deeply moved by their plight. His sense of injustice is so inflamed that a spark is ignited and he hits and kills the Egyptian oppressor. Passion yields to action, and a forceful and irrevocable one at that. The next day, transformed by the previous day's experience, he is now able, with further clarity of vision, to see that even within his brethren, injustice is occurring. This time, however, his passion leads to an action that is far more measured. He calls out sharply to the clearly identified "wicked one" in an attempt to stop him from hitting his fellow Hebrew. Upon reflection between Day One and Day Two, Moses appears to have learned that his passion need not consume him. Yet, his intervention has a startling consequence. This wicked one rebuffs Moses, questioning his very right to pass judgment. Moreover, he reveals that he is aware that the day before Moses struck and killed the Egyptian. Moses has no response to either the wicked one or to the other Hebrew and retreats inward, fearful that all of Egypt now knows of his impassioned action of Day One. And the text immediately substantiates Moses' fear. Pharaoh himself becomes aware of what Moses has done and seeks to kill him, now no longer a protected prince and grandson, but a common fugitive. So Moses flees to the land of Midian, where he dwells.

Our next immediate encounter with Moses shows him being confronted with yet a third incident of injustice to which he responds.

> Now the chief of Midian had seven daughters, and they came and drew [water], and they filled the troughs to water their father's flocks. But the shepherds came and drove them away; so Moses arose and rescued them and watered their flocks. They came to their father Reuel, and he said, Why have you come so quickly today? They replied, An Egyptian man rescued us from the hand[s]

of the shepherds, and he also drew [water] for us and watered the flocks. (Exod 2:16–19)

Several things emerge. Moses has not lost his sense of injustice, nor has he lost his ability to take action to rectify the situation. And it is more measured than his earlier [Day One in Egypt] action of killing the Egyptian. He chooses, however, not to attempt to use any verbal communication as his means, for his Day Two experience in Egypt has hampered his ability to literally speak out against injustice. And finally, he is identified by Jethro's daughters simply and solely as "an Egyptian man." That he was not recognizable as a Hebrew is perhaps understandable. But the daughters don't say "a brave man," "a kind man," "a righteous man," or even "a stranger." He is sufficiently knowable to them, now having so submerged his albeit-confused and merged identity as son of Pharaoh's daughter/newly identified Hebrew, that he is distinctly "an Egyptian man." His reward, however, for his intervention is Jethro's hospitality, culminating with marriage to Zipporah and what then appears to be a comfortable life as shepherd and son-in-law to the High Priest of Midian.

God apparently had other plans, which brings us back to the encounter with the burning bush. Why did God set up this elaborate and miraculous occurrence for Moses? The bush, you'll recall, contained within it a flame in which there was an angel of God. And the bush, while burning, was not fully consumed by the flame as might otherwise be expected. Perhaps this burning bush was supposed to be a sign to Moses about reaching inward to find his inner passion and flame. It was a message to see that there is an inner, God-inspired call to action, to both speak out and act out against injustice. And these calls-to-action can be operationalized in ways that allow you to act without losing yourself in, or being destroyed by, the passion of your response. The burning bush was to serve as a metaphor for what was Moses' potential, if only he would look with clarity of vision. And yet, Moses' vision, as is often the case with many of us, was obscured. Not too obscured to have lost that spark that enabled him to see that there was something wondrous that he was encountering. But sufficiently obscured, sufficiently unconsciously frightening, that he couldn't even see the bush burning, acknowledge his own passion, for fear that it would lead to his destruction. It is for this reason that the angel of God was insufficient for the task and God had to call out to Moses directly.

And what does God say to Moses?

> And He said, "I am the God of your father, the God of Abraham, the God of Isaac, and the God of Jacob." And Moses hid his face because he was afraid to look toward God. (Exod 3:6)

God in effect says, You must know and acknowledge who you are: who your ancestors were, what passions drove them to speak out against injustice and to act in righteous ways, and how that history informs who you should be as a righteous individual. When Moses turns his head from God, I would suggest that it is because, in this one statement, he realized that his fears had led him to be seen only as "an Egyptian man." Yes, he was acting in a righteous manner, but his behavior could not be seen within the context of his individual or larger historic ties to righteousness as a member of the Jewish people. And God further reinforces this message by indicating that running from injustice, as Moses did, doesn't make injustice disappear. So during this whole time, while Moses no longer saw the afflictions of his people, i.e. "out of sight, out of mind," it is God who reminds him:

> I have surely seen the affliction of My people who are in Egypt, and I have heard their cry because of their slave drivers, for I know their pains. I have descended to rescue them from the hand[s] of the Egyptians and to bring them up from that land, to a good and spacious land, to a land flowing with milk and honey, to the place of the Canaanites, the Hittites, the Amorites, the Perizzites, the Hivvites, and the Jebusites. And now, behold, the cry of the children of Israel has come to Me, and I have also seen the oppression that the Egyptians are oppressing them. So now come, and I will send you to Pharaoh, and take My people, the children of Israel, out of Egypt. (Exod 3:7–12)

The issue is not whether there is injustice in the world, nor whether God sees the injustice and acts. The challenge for Moses, as it was for Abraham, Isaac, Jacob, Sarah, Rebecca, Rachel and Leah, and as it was and is for all generations, is what do we see, what do we say and what do we do. The lesson of the burning bush is that there is, and there always will be, a burning bush. That is our internal, eternal flame, calling us to action as individuals and collectively as Jews, on behalf of all those who are oppressed and afflicted. It is a statement that says we have a covenantal-commanding Law and a three thousand year history, which require us to always pursue righteousness, even in the face of individual or collective adversity. The burning bush calls out to us to summon-up our God-like abilities. We are challenged to not be afraid to acknowledge our identity, our history and to see them as reflective of the commanding presence of God. If we succeed, we can then act with passion in righteous ways without being consumed or destroyed in the process. Then we will have incorporated that burning bush, that spark and flame of righteousness, into our very fabric and character.

8

REVELATION AT SINAI
THE FORECAST IS FOR CLOUDS AND SMOKE

THE STORY OF THE revelation at Mount Sinai, recounted grandly in Exodus in Chapters 19–20, is perhaps the defining moment for the Jewish people. There are three days of preparation, after which Moses ascends the mountain amidst much sound and fury. On the mountaintop he encounters God, who reveals the words of the Torah. Our sages have warned that we should not consider this encounter limited to a specific historic moment, one we recall in the cycle of the public Torah readings and commemorate on the holiday of *Shavuot*, Pentecost. Rather, it is intended to be a daily new experience/re-experience in which we actively engage and participate. What we learn from the first revelation at Mount Sinai can help direct our focus as we face the formidable challenge of making revelation alive anew each day.

We are taught as children that the reason God chose Mount Sinai as the place of revelation was that it was the smallest of all the mountains, reflecting the importance of humility. The late Lubavitcher Rebbe, Rabbi Menachem Mendel Schneerson, noted [in public discourses] that another crucial aspect of this chosen mountain is that it was located in a desert. Just as the desert has no owner, God's choice of the desert as the site of revelation indicates that no one person or tribe has ownership of revelation; every Jew has an equal claim to Torah. Following along this theme, the *Midrash*[1], in its explanation of the words "But with the one who is here with us standing today before God and those who are not here among us today" (Deut 29:14)—which is part of a recounting of the revelation—tells us that the souls of all the members of our people throughout the generations were present at Mount Sinai.[2] Each and every Jew owns a piece of the revelatory experience. But what occurred, what was the nature of that revelatory experience in which all Jewish souls were participants, and how did that core experience impact on us for generations to come?

As described in the Torah, it was Moses who had a unique face-to-face encounter with God, and achieved a level of closeness that none of us will ever attain. For the rest of the Jewish people, present and or future, that primal collective Jewish revelatory experience, however, was not one of great clarity. We stood at the base of the mountain, and it was

> . . .becoming morning, there was thunder and lightning and a heavy cloud on the mountain . . .Mount Sinai was smoking in its entirety because God had descended upon it in the fire; its smoke ascended like the smoke of the lime pit . . . (Exod 19:16, 18)

Dr. Ismar Schorsch, Biblical scholar, has written that "God remains inscrutable. Revelation in the Torah occurs time and again in a setting obscured by darkness."[3]

I find all this to be a somewhat puzzling contrast to the comment in the *Mechilta* (a mostly legal Midrashic collection on the book of Exodus) on the pre-revelation experience at the sea, the famed *Shirat HaYam*, the Song at the Sea, which Moses sings immediately following the salvation of the Jews through God's splitting of the Red Sea and the drowning of the Egyptians. On the words ". . . This is my God . . ." (Exod 15:2) the comment is made

1. The genre of rabbinic interpretive tradition of stories, parables and legal exegesis on Biblical texts. All subsequent citations from the various Midrashic texts are available online in the original text at Sefaria.org.

2. Midrash *Tanchuma* 3, cited by Rashi on Deut.29:14.

3. Schorsch, "Chancellor's Parashah Commentary," p.1.

"A servant girl saw at the sea that which Isaiah, Ezekiel and all the other prophets did not behold."[4] Do we thus understand that the peak theological experience took place at the Red Sea and by the time of the revelation at Sinai there was some decline in the capacity to experience God? Perhaps it is worthwhile to compare and contrast the very nature of the two miraculous events and also the differences between a servant girl and an established prophet.

At the banks of the Red Sea, the Jewish people found themselves between the proverbial "rock and a hard place." The Egyptian army, chariots and soldiers led by the Pharaoh himself were bearing down upon them, and on the other side there was a sea that spelled certain death as well. God commands Moses to tell the people to literally move and he will split the Sea and save them. And that is exactly what occurs as the Egyptians, their chariots and horses are all drowned by the waters that return after the Jewish people miraculously go through the sea to safety on the other side (Exod 14:15–31). On the most primitive of levels, we understand our primary need and desire for survival and can recognize when something has occurred that delivers such an unanticipated salvation. This met-need is however, perhaps the most egocentric, self-serving narcissistic need that we have. It is "help ME, save ME." And after such an event, it is easy to understand that a very primitive sense of gratitude to the savior is easily evoked, with a glib willingness to label that savior "This is MY God and I will glorify . . ." This is not fundamentally a complex nor a nuanced relationship; rather, simply it says "Meet my need and I see You and acknowledge You." Thus even the servant girl had great capacity to see the [simple] hand of a saving God. The prophets, hundreds of years later, were dealing with the complexities of a now long-established people in a now long-established and far more complex relationship with a God who had demanding and commanding

---

4. Rashi on Exod.15:3, citing the *Mechilta*. This legend assumes that there was some hierarchical structure functioning even among the enslaved Jewish people such that we can meaningfully refer to someone post-exodus as a "servant."

expectations for morality, righteousness, and faithfulness, all of which were frequently unmet by the Jewish people.

But now let's look at this issue from a radically different perspective. How might it be possible to value the experience of the servant girl at the time of the splitting of the Red Sea as, in fact, a far more profound sense of experiencing God than we were able to have at Sinai, and beyond that which all the prophets were able to have? The key may be in the unusual reference of the *Mechilta* to a "servant girl." The comment would still have its intended message ostensibly if it said, "the average person" or "a young boy or girl." A servant is by definition one who is humbled by virtue of his/her position in relationship to another. Narcissistic, egocentric needs do not and cannot take precedence. In fact, the essence of being a "good" servant is to perhaps anticipate the other's need, and if not, certainly to be listening for the articulation of a need from the other before one pursues one's own needs. An established prophet, whether you view him/her as being called upon by God or self-proclaiming him/herself as called upon by God, is always in a defined state of being both close to God and holier to some extent than the "common" man or woman.

So who are we called upon to be, as we reflect upon ourselves within the historic collective story of The Revelation, while seeking daily our own personalized revelation? If I blend the earlier Exodus experience of the servant girl at the Red Sea with the picture of clouds, smoke, and obscured vision of Mount Sinai, and the position of prophet, we may find ourselves seated within the circle of theological modesty. I am called upon as a function of a commanding relationship with God, whether viewed through the lens of revelation or simply by virtue of my existence in this world as a human being, to pursue morality and righteousness. I dare not, however, view myself as the designated prophet of God, holier than all others and more knowing of God. Like the servant girl, I exist as a humble servant and need to be prepared to not simply listen to my own voice but to be sensitive to, and listen to the voices of, others. It is not with a clear sense of vision that I approach this. Inevitably, I will stumble in the darkness, a darkness at times of my own creation. But I must daily struggle to find God's presence in my life, in the world and in others, seeking to identify that Divine spark in them which I want others to see in me.

9

SHABBAT AS A MODEL FOR THEOLOGICAL MODESTY

THE DICTIONARY OFFERS NO less than forty definitions for the word "work."[1] The very first definition gets to the heart of what I think most of us understand when we use the term: "exertion or effort directed to produce or accomplish something; labor; toil." It is often hard for many people, unless otherwise raised within a very traditional and/or Orthodox Jewish worldview, to understand the various prohibitions of *melachot*, types of work activities that are deemed forbidden to do on the Sabbath (*Shabbat*). The first of many textual references is found in the first account of the giving of the Ten Commandments at Mount Sinai, in the book of Exodus, where the fourth commandment states:

> Remember[2] the Sabbath day to make it holy. Six days you shall work and do all your *melachot* ["work"]. And the seventh day is Sabbath for the Lord your God. You shall not do any *melacha* [work], you, and your son, and your daughter, your servant and your maidservant, and

1. Random House College Dictionary, Revised edition, 1976, p.1516.

2. A review of the second accounting of the Ten Commandments in Deuteronomy Ch.5:12–15 is also useful. There the opening commanding word is not the *Zachor*, "remember" of our Exodus account, but rather *Shamor*, "guard" which is rabbinically seen as even more focused on the prohibitions and laws necessary to preserve the observance of the Sabbath.

your animal and your alien who is within your gates. Because for six days God made the heavens and the earth and the ocean and all that is in it, and on the seventh day [God] rested. Therefore God blessed the seventh day and sanctified it. (Exod 20:8–11)

Because God stopped working we must also stop working. In essence we are called upon to be God-like. It is our place in this world to toil productively and to cease from working, and apparently to also "rest." Let's first try to understand the notion of *melacha*, work.

Mishnaic and subsequent Talmudic rabbinic interpretation start with thirty-nine broad categories of activities that were all involved in the construction of the Tabernacle and from that derive hundreds of sub-categories. Two thousand years of rabbinic interpretation has resulted in the promulgation of thousands of rulings and prohibitions, and even legal work-arounds (all puns intended) to make the forbidden permissible. Some seem to have aspects of the exertion, labor, effort and toil we commonly associate with "work," while so many others seem to be devoid of that quality. One need only look at issues of turning on electric lights or ways to cut and serve a grapefruit while dealing with its internal seeds to see examples of the non-exertive yet prohibited work we call *melacha*. So we need to find larger, thematic principles that will help us to understand this concept more profoundly.

While there are a variety of ways to conceptualize *melacha*, "work," the two I find most compelling are related to creative mastery over nature and mastery over fellow human beings.[3] There is a rabbinical prohibition against riding or even making use of an animal's body on the Sabbath or a Festival Day (Babylonian Talmud,[4] *Beitza* 19a). The reason given by the Talmud is a concern that one may break off a tree branch, deemed to be a biblical violation of the Sabbath, in order to strike the animal while leading it along

3. See, for example, Heschel, A. *The Sabbath.*

4. All subsequent references to the Talmud, unless otherwise noted, refer to the Babylonian Talmud. The full text is available online at Sefaria.org in the original Aramaic.

or riding it. Breaking this branch needn't involve a major effort of exertion, and would equally apply to a small branch or even a twig. On the Sabbath, I am called upon to view my animal not as a beast of burden for my free use but to see it as a part of God's creations. I am required to facilitate for my animal a twenty-five hour period of rest that is the same as I am allocated. And the tree, which during the week I can use in any way (e.g. snap a branch to use to prod my animal, or cut it down for lumber or to fashion toothpicks), it too is a part of God's creations. I am called upon for a day to step back with humility and to abdicate my illusory crown as the pinnacle of God's creations.

With regard to my mastery over others, Rabbi Shai Held, philosopher, teacher and author, has written: "One of the most radical ideas in all of Jewish law is the insistence that we may not handle money on the Sabbath. On the Sabbath, both the richest of the rich and the poorest of the poor leave their wallets at home; the billionaire and the poor gas station attendant are totally equal. The message is clear: Socio-economic status tells us nothing about metaphysical status."[5] This aspect of the Sabbath tells us that we need to step back from our illusory places of status, position and rank in comparison to our fellow human beings. There is God, and then all of humanity exists equally on Shabbat, by virtue of an act of God's grace.

But we still must examine yet the other aspect of the Sabbath, for it is not only that we are enjoined to be God-like by ceasing and desisting from "work." We are also called upon to" rest." And later in Exodus we are offered yet another aspect of what the Sabbath remarkably seems to afford to God. There we are told:

> And the children of Israel will observe the Sabbath, to make the Sabbath for their generations as an eternal covenant. Between me and the children of Israel it is a sign for all eternity. For [in] six days God made the heavens and the earth and on the seventh day [God] rested and

5. Mechon Hadar newsletter, April 2014 "Another World to Live In: The Meaning of Shabbat" Iyar 5744.

[God] was refreshed/[God's] soul was renewed. (Exod 31:16–17)

Now we need to ask ourselves, "Is it enough to simply cease working? Have I "remembered" (the *Zachor* of the commandment in Exodus) and "guarded" (the *Shamor* of the second account in Deuteronomy) such that I have fulfilled the essence of observance of the Sabbath? And even further, if I refrain from work and I rest but I don't experience some sense of refreshment, or a renewal of my soul, have I fulfilled my obligation to be God-like in my observance?

Rabbi Samuel Blech, of blessed memory, the Rabbi of the Fur Center Synagogue in New York City which my family attended when I was a teenager, once quoted an unusual statement in the Talmud:

R. Johanan said: Three are those who will inherit the world to come: those who dwell in the Land of Israel; and those who bring up their children to the study of the Torah; and those who recite *Havdalah* [literally "separation;" a ritual involving wine, spices and a candle at the end of the Sabbath] over wine at the termination of the Sabbath. Who is that? Those who leave over [wine] from *Kiddush* [ritual with blessing over wine at the onset of the Sabbath] for *Havdalah*. (Talmud, *Pesachim* 113a)

Rabbi Blech acknowledged the extraordinary value placed by the sages of the Talmud on settling in the land of Israel and also of teaching one's children Torah. Each of these acts, at various points, are deemed to be equivalent to observing all the other commandments in their entirety. But what was the importance of leaving over some wine from the Friday night *Kiddush* to be used the following evening at the *Havdalah*, when we bid goodbye to the Sabbath and we can return to our work states of mastery and dominance over nature and others? Rabbi Blech offered the insight that the Sabbath comes to teach us lessons that we need to actively and purposefully carry over into our "work" week if we are truly to be God-like and experience this sense of refreshment and renewal.

So what can we do in the realms of mastery over nature and over our fellow human beings so that we incorporate this precious Sabbath/God-like perspective into the week? For one, we might choose to reframe our position in this world with regard to animals and the environment as one in which we are partners with God and serve as stewards of the physical universe, responsible for seeing that we responsibly use it and not abuse it; protect it and respect it. We have far too many examples of ways in which we are destroying our environment and other species as we pursue "development" with abandon. We act this way and allow others to act this way because of arrogance. We view ourselves as owners of the physical environment, as opposed to toilers or even day laborers in God's universe.

We also need to figure out alternative models for interacting with our fellow human beings throughout the week, that are not based on illusory distinctions of wealth, status, rank and position. Certainly in the United States and throughout the world, the gap between the "haves" and the "have-nots" continues to widen, and with it we see a desensitization to the needs and the plight of others. The traditional approach to Jewish burial has all of us, regardless of wealth or status, being buried in a simple, plain wooden coffin. And we are all to be buried in the same array of *tachrichim*, shrouds—and there are no pockets in shrouds, as the old Jewish joke goes. We will be equal in death as we are all lowered into, and return to, the earth. But we have a greater opportunity to actively realize our potential, our God-like qualities, now, in our lives. Literally and symbolically, take some of that Sabbath wine and save it for the full week, allowing its humanizing and humbling perspective to enable us to have our souls nourished and refreshed.

10

"AND THEY SHALL MAKE ME A SANCTUARY"
WHO HAS THE BUILDING PERMIT?

AMONG THE MANY FAMOUS quotations that often appear some-where above the Ark, one of the most popular is taken from the book of Exodus.

> And they shall make unto me a sanctuary and I will dwell
> in their midst. (Exod 25:8)

It would be easy to read this in a limited sense regarding the sanctuary built in the wilderness within the context of the various sentences that precede and then follow this verse. But within our tradition, up through and including modern times, we tend to see this as broad statement about God's presence in the holy places we create. This seems to suggest the possibility of God requiring some defined space in which to be present to us, and that said space also must be constructed with the intention of it being a holy place in which God will dwell, i.e. if we construct a place as a holy place, as a sanctuary for God's dwelling, only then will God be present. Thus, one could think that we might have difficulty and/or be precluded from experiencing God in the absence of our active, intentional creation of such a holy, defined space.

Compare and contrast this with a sentence from Genesis, one which we have previously discussed in Chapter 5. When Jacob awakens from his dream of the angels ascending and descending, he states,

> Surely God is in this place and I, I did not know. And he was fearful/awe-struck and he said, How wondrous is this place! Surely this is nothing less than the house of God and this is the gate to heaven. (Gen 28:16–17)

Jacob also seems to have had a concept of God being situated in a place. He boldly proclaims, albeit after-the-fact, that said place was the house of God and the gate to heaven, perhaps to the exclusion of God possibly being in another place, either at that time or at any time! Our job, which Jacob acknowledges he failed to do, is to be cognizant of God's presence. So while the issue of intentionality may have some relevance, we are still dealing with a defined special place for God, in which we can choose to/may be cognizant of God—or not.

King David, in the book of Psalms, appears to give a different view of God's presence, at least initially.

> Unto God is the earth and its fullness, the entire world and all its inhabitants (Ps 24:1)

But then he too reverts to the language of a "place."

> Who shall go up to the mountain of God and who will be established in His [God's] holy place? The one who is clean of hands and pure of heart, who has not lifted up my soul in vain and has not sworn deceitfully. (Ps 24:3–4)

Rabbi Samson Raphael Hirsch, nineteenth-century German rabbinic leader and scholar, comments on the above verse in Psalms and suggests that with the totality of the earth being God's, EVERY place is the mountain of God and EVERY place is therefore potentially a holy place.[1] It is evocative of the famed saying attributed to the Kotzker Rebbe, "Where do you find God?

---

1. Hirsch, *The Psalms*, p. 174.

Wherever you let Him in." In fact, one of the most commonly used terms to refer to God is *HaMakom*, literally "the place."

What sense are we to make of all of this? We started this book with the Kabbalistic notion of *tzimtzum*, of God's need [sic] to willfully contract His presence in order for anything or anyone else to even exist. This notion suggests a limitation, a containment of God's essence as being the essential precursor to anything and everything. Human intentionality is irrelevant at this stage—but as our Torah begins with that very act of *Tzimtzum* having already been accomplished, God's intentionality and purposefulness is apparent, exemplary of God's grace. Once God has set this in motion, then we can create intentional spaces and places that may assist us to be aware of God's presence. We can be anyplace in God's world and experience God if we allow ourselves to, regardless of the location or the structure or the intentionality that brought us to that place or brought us to create that structure. Our lives, however long or short, are a series of connected moments in time in which we can choose to be aware of and open to God's presence, or not. For some of us, and at some times, we may find that our awareness is best facilitated within the formal physical setting of a synagogue and within the defined structures of a prayer or worship service. For others it may be when we are immersed in the grandeur and beauty of this world. A glorious hike on a mountain or a walk on the beach with a vista of a seemingly endless ocean and horizon may best speak to us and enable us to realize that we are in God's presence and have been at all times.

King David, in the previous quote from Psalm 24, gives us a window into understanding what we may need to do to maximize our openness to the experience of God.

> The one who is clean of hands and pure of heart, who has not lifted up my soul in vain and has not sworn deceitfully.

How are we to be "clean of hands" or "pure of heart?" What does it mean that we have not lifted up "My soul" in vain, where the "My" is referring to God as the ultimate owner of that soul?

And who among us can even say that we have not at some time "sworn deceitfully?"

Let me suggest that we can begin to meet these criteria when we actively seek out the best ways to be personally open to and experience God, while not coming with full-hands, i.e. carrying the baggage of certainty of what we think we know is the right way or the right place. We need to understand that God has given every human being a soul, in effect a piece of God's soul or essence, for us to use in purposeful ways to connect to, and with, God. And perhaps we "swear deceitfully" if our quest to find and experience God really masks our attempts to define how others are looking for God in all the wrong places.

We all need to find that place and time within that enables us to find and acknowledge God. Who has the "building permit?" We all do. From the moment we are born until we die, we each have one. The name on the permit is our own name, and we cannot really "build a sanctuary" in the most profound sense for anyone but ourselves. We can share with others what approaches or perspectives, or rituals or activities at times work best for us. We are not, however the inspectors for any structures other than those that we have created for ourselves, be they literal or metaphorical. We certainly do not issue the certificates of occupancy for anyone but ourselves. And it's a long-term lease, not a one-time purchase. Daily we need to tend to our own houses, renovating, rehabilitating and building ever-expanding places within our souls in which to welcome God's presence.

SECTION III

GOD CALLS AND OUR CALLING

11

KORBAN: YOU CAN'T OFFER THAT WHICH YOU DON'T POSSESS

UNDERSTANDING THE ENTIRE SACRIFICIAL system is at best difficult for most twenty-first century Jews. The complexities and the
nuances of the sacrificial order and system range from daily sacrifices, sacrifices for the Sabbath and holidays, voluntary sacrifices of
thanksgiving and sacrifices related to atonement for specific sins.
Even classical commentators, most notably Maimonides[1] and
Nachmanides,[2] differed on their views regarding the entire original intent of God's commandments related to the sacrificial order.
Maimonides saw the purpose as related to "weaning" the Jewish
people away from what was a common-place, less-than-optimal
pagan approach to serving God, while Nachmanides framed it in a
far more positive light as a desired approach to serving God.

One of the difficulties in understanding this entire subject is
inherent in the English translation of the word *korban* as "sacrifice." The Hebrew word *Korban,* whose root is *k-r-v,* relates to the
concept of drawing near. Regardless of the type and purpose of the
specific *korban,* the overall goal of the entire system was in some
way to bring the individual or the Jewish people closer to God. The

1. Rabbi Moses ben Maimon (1135–1204), preeminent Medieval Spanish
Jewish scholar and philosopher.

2. Rabbi Moses ben Naḥman Girondi (1194–1270), leading medieval Jewish scholar, philosopher and biblical commentator.

opening lines of the book of Leviticus can shed some light on this purpose, and perhaps enable us to examine the parameters that should define the ways in which we can attempt to become closer to God.

> Speak to the children of Israel. And you shall say to them. A human [Hebrew: *adam*] from whom you will make an offering to God . . . " (Lev 1:2)

Rashi raises a question, noting that the Torah uses the term *Adam*, as opposed to *ish*, "a man," and says, quoting from the Midrash *Vayikra Rabba*[3] (Chr 2:7):

> Why is it [Adam] said? [To teach us that] just like Adam [the first] did not bring sacrifices or offerings from that which was stolen, since everything was "available" to him, so to you should not bring offerings from anything that has been stolen.

An interesting question, with a remarkable answer. The answer is not remarkable for its apparent legal implications regarding requiring appropriate ownership of any animal, bird, grains or other products to be used for a sacrificial offering. Rather, it is astonishing because it casually asserts a sweeping statement about Adam, ignoring the reality, which was that almost everything was available to him. When placed in the Garden of Eden, the only thing that Adam and Eve were expressly forbidden to eat from was the Tree of Knowledge, good and evil. Not everything was available to Adam, and in fact there was this one thing that would have been considered stolen or inappropriate for Adam to use in an offering. How do we then relate this above-referenced Midrash to the underlying meta-message of the sacrificial system as a device to bring us closer to God?

Earlier in this book, I suggested that the danger presented by the Tree of Knowledge, and thus the prohibition against eating its fruit, was related to the potential for Adam and Eve to erroneously believe that they would have God-like knowledge, knowledge of God, and

---

3. One of the older Midrashic collections, 5th century CE, noted for its homiletic expository sermons based on weekly Torah portions.

know God's motives and intents. This distortion of boundaries, with its concomitant arrogance that falsely asserts that humans can have some God-like knowledge of ultimate truth regarding that which is good or evil, is precisely that which cannot be a part of our sacrificial offering. It represents the antithesis of the attitude necessary to become closer to God, whether in regularly scheduled offerings, those which are thanksgiving offerings, and certainly ones in which we seek atonement for a sin. With this in mind, let us now re-interpret the quote cited above from *Vayikra Rabba*:

> Why is it [Adam] said? [To teach us that] just like Adam [the first] could bring an offering from everything that was available to him to possess – except by claiming to possess the Ultimate Truth – so too we cannot attempt to come closer to God by claiming to possess the Ultimate Truth.

None of us has a right to claim an inherent advantage in becoming closer to God by virtue of our beliefs, practices or faith. None of us starts at an advantaged position of being closer to God by virtue of these either. Regardless of the type of *korban* we are bringing, each time we are in effect Adam the "first". Becoming closer to God is the challenge that lies before us. All we can know is what we have done and how we may feel or not feel after this offering of ourselves. We do not receive the immediate feedback we see God providing in Genesis to the offerings brought by Cain and Abel. We can know what we feel, but whether God senses a greater closeness remains a question, the answer to which only God knows.

12

TZARAAT ON A HOUSE
THE POTENTIAL FOR TRANSFORMATION

MANY OF US GREW up with the classical English translation of the word *tzaraat* in the Torah, particularly in the portions of *Tazria* and *Metzora* in Leviticus, having been translated as "leprosy." Whatever this skin affliction was or was supposed to be understood to be, there is a rich tradition of commentaries associating it with a God-given affliction as punishment for speaking *lashon hara*, speaking badly, albeit truthfully, about another person. The archetype for this is when Miriam and Aaron speak badly of their brother Moses' action of taking a Cushite woman as his wife and also question Moses' authority. In Numbers (12:1–15), the story unfolds and Miriam is afflicted with *tzaraat*, requiring a seven-day period of sequestration from the overall camp before she could return and then journey with the people.[1]

But what do we make of the passages in Leviticus, which describe a manifestation of this *tzaraat* on the walls of a house, also known in the Talmud as the *bayit hamenuga*, the plagued house?

> And God spoke to Moses and Aaron saying. When you come into the land of Canaan that I shall give to you as a

---

1. Whether *tzaraat* is seen as a God-induced affliction or some psychosomatization by the individual him/herself related to an emotional issue is a subject worthy of the considerable discussions that exist on the topic

possession and I will give the plague of *tzaraat* in a house in the land of your possession. And the one to whom the house belongs shall come and tell to the Priest saying, It appears to me like a plague in the house. (Lev 14:33–35)

Even at this early stage several questions emerge that bear consideration. Unlike the *tzaraat* that afflicts an individual which can occur outside the land of Canaan, later called Israel, this affliction appears to pertain only to structures that are in the land that God will give, i.e. has not yet given, nor have the people even arrived there, much less taken possession of the land. This could appear to be some sort of warning about potentials that could come or are likely to come. Secondly, it appears that the relationship of the person to the house in question is one of ownership or possession; a renter of a house might well be excluded from the scenario and laws associated with this whole passage. And note the specific language, "And the one to whom the house belongs says, It appears to me like a plague in the house." This seems to imply that the most important determinant of the potential severity of the situation is the individual owner, who at this early stage has sufficient perspective to go to the Priest on his/her own initiative to express concern.

In the ensuing passages in the chapter, there is a description of the Priest's investigation of the house. There are specific possible signs of *tzaraat* on the walls, with regard to both the nature and color of the plague, as well as the depth to which this affliction seems to be within the very walls and stones of the house itself. Two possibilities emerge. In the first scenario, described in verses 37–42, the plague appears to afflict certain stones such that they can be removed and the house declared impure for seven days, after which new stones are inserted and a new coating is placed over the walls and the house is deemed suitable to be re-inhabited. In the second scenario, the Priest, upon returning after the initial seven day period, determines that the plague has in fact spread throughout the house, like a malignancy, such that the entire house—its walls, stones, wood and dust—must be destroyed (verses 43–47).

Many questions about this entire situation and the contained commandments could be raised. But I would rather focus on a rather astonishing assertion in the Talmud, that this "plagued house" is one of three commandments given in the Torah that are deemed "*lo hayah, v'lo yehiyeh*," they never were nor will they ever be. This notion as understood in the Talmud (*Sanhedrin*, 71a) suggests that these laws were given to provide merit to those who would study them and thereby derive from them an underlying ethical/moral/spiritual teaching that would have a profound and perhaps overarching impact on one's behavior.[2] A brief summary of the other two commandments are in order if we are to understand what the unifying themes are and what lessons we can learn specifically from our case of the house with *tzaraat*.

In Deut 13:13–18, we have the commandment regarding a city which has been completely subverted from following God's ways, called the *ir nidachat*. The intricacies of the situation require that: the agents of this mass apostasy be at least two adult males from the tribe to which the city belonged; the followers must be at least the majority of the adult males of the city; the overall population of the city must be at least one hundred but smaller than the tribe's majority; every single involved individual was forewarned appropriately and given the chance to repent and failed to do so; and, only the "Great Sanhedrin"[3] could identify/pronounce such a city as fitting all these conditions. The punishment was to kill all the inhabitants of the city and all its animals by the sword, then to take all the spoils of the city to a central place and burn them. Following that, the entire city is to be burnt to the ground. The former site of this city is one on which a city shall never again be built, and it is to remain a living testament to the consequences of violating God's laws. The likelihood of all the above-referenced conditions being met were seen by most in the Talmud to be so impossible as

2. A fascinating and in-depth presentation and analysis of these three commandments can be found in Gevrayahu & Sicherman, "What Never Was and Never Will Be," 2001.

3. The Great Sanhedrin refers to the Rabbinical Court of 71 Judges which served as the equivalent of a Supreme Court, and functioned during the periods of the First and Second Temples and up through the middle of the 4th century CE.

to place the entire commandment in the category of "never was and never will be."

In Deut 21:18–21, we have the commandment regarding the *ben sorrer umoreh*, the rebellious child. Here too, we have an example of extremism and excess, although of a very different nature than above. A man presents himself to the elders of his city and declares that his son [classically this is seen as only applying to a male child] doesn't listen to the voice of his father and the voice of his mother. Despite all reprimands he doesn't obey them and he is additionally a glutton and a drunkard. All the people of the city are then required to participate in the stoning of the young man, as part of a communal effort to eradicate evil, resulting in all the inhabitants subsequently listening to and fearing [God's ways]. In the rabbinic understanding of this otherwise rather shocking display of parental and communal discipline, there are a variety of conditions that are necessary to meet the standard of being a "rebellious child." There was a very proscribed age for the child, and a highly defined and limited time period in which the behaviors could occur. The amounts of food and alcohol required to have been consumed was excessive and the interval in which this consumption occurred was also narrowly defined. The number of warnings required were multiple and had to be of the same nature, and both mother and father had to independently indict their child for his behaviors, but use the exact same words to describe his behavior. Here too, the Rabbis of the Talmud saw this case as *lo hayah v'lo yehiyeh*—never was and never will be.

So, what are the common themes here? In each of the three cases there is a level of pervasive and invasive evil that seems to threaten the larger community of Israel as a whole. And while there are indications that at intermediate stages we are hopeful of intervention that will avoid the inevitable, each has as a final outcome a total destruction and eradication. In the case of the house, it is a house that is completely eradicated. In the cases of the subverted city and the rebellious child however, we are annihilating human (and animal) life. If we are to take these texts as written, they seem to speak to a level of evil and wrong-doing that crosses the line between redeemable and forever unredeemable. When viewed through the lens of the Talmudic statement of "never was and never will be" however, a radically different message emerges that has the potential to teach us ethical, moral and spiritual lessons about ourselves and our consideration of others.

Let us return to the focus of this chapter, the *bayit hamenuga*, the house afflicted with a pervasive malignancy of some form. In the opening I raised the issue as to why this situation speaks only to a future time at which we as a people will become the possessors of another people's land. When one owns something, much less owns something in a land that once belonged to others and experiences this new-found power of possession and ownership as God-given, we are being alerted that we are already in a "danger zone" with potential for excess and the associated arrogance, hubris and dismissal of others. But we need not limit our thinking here to a literal house, a literal physical structure. As I suggest in a later chapter (Ch. 21, "Why We Need Railings Around the Roofs of Our Houses"), "house" can refer to the concepts and ideas that we construct and hold dear. Our situation here in Leviticus speaks to the ways in which we can be fortunate enough to discover through insight, introspection and some painful soul-searching, that I have something that resembles a plague in my house. I'm on the path to creating some invasive and pervasive state of personal malignancy for which I bear responsibility. It may be of an intellectual, theological or emotional nature. My concerns are such that I also know that I need the help of a "priest"—perhaps a friend, family member, therapist, spiritual mentor or guide. I know that I need someone to help me identify and address the issue at an early stage. Only then will remediation and rehabilitation be possible that will lead to my being "redeemable," as well as capable of reintegration into the larger community that I wish to be a part of and whose acceptance I desire.

But what of our message of "it never was and never will be?" I think that the lesson is one that says that we have no right to ever give up hope about the ability of people to transform themselves. There may be a "house," a "child," a "city" that appears to be beyond hope, beyond redemption, beyond transformation because of an inherent, pervasive and malignant evil. The Torah instructs us to go back and look again, and find some way to view this differently, for it is not beyond hope, transformation or redemption. It is our individual and communal duty when confronted with these situations, be it internally or in others, to understand the problem, to identify the sources and to struggle to create possible solutions. "It never was and never will be" places an awesome responsibility upon us precisely because there is never to be a point at which we can justify throwing up our hands, abandoning hope and simply looking to eradicate, obliterate and eliminate that which is before us. Nothing, no one is beyond redemption. Perhaps we need to acknowledge our own failings and short-comings if we are unable to realize the potential for redemption in ourselves or others. We must recognize that we are all potentially that "house," that "child," or that "city" in need of help to deal with our failings and short-comings. Simultaneously, we can all be the "priest" or the "elders," the one who extends a helping hand and wise counsel. On a global note, we bear responsibility for recognizing when we seem to be headed toward a danger zone of uncontrolled and excessive evils. And we must extend our hands and counsel to others to help find solutions that avoid eradication, obliteration of others because we've so boldly deemed them beyond redemption. And if we get to such a point that it appears that the other is beyond redemption, then at least we must bear responsibility for allowing a situation to fester to point that was intended to *lo haya v'lo yehiyeh*—never was and never will be.

13

"YOU SHALL BE HOLY BECAUSE I AM HOLY"

THAT'S THE BIG PICTURE?

THE TORAH PORTION KNOWN as *Kedoshim* ("Holy") begins with the following:

> And God spoke to Moses saying. Speak unto the entire congregation of the children of Israel and say to them. You shall be holy because I am holy, YHVH, your God. (Lev 19:1–2)

A friend once told me that a prominent rabbi suggested that this was the "real" mid-point to the Torah. There are in fact numerous approaches to determining the "middle of the Torah" with differing viewpoints and some more broadly accepted views, calculated by the numbers of total letters, words, or phrases or verses. This sentence, however, doesn't actually find its way into any of these calculations as the midpoint. So what did this distinguished rabbi mean? From his perspective, with all the commandments about specific ritual and civil laws that start in Exodus and run through Leviticus and continue on into Numbers and Deuteronomy as well, this sentence comes as a "speed bump" in the road. It says to us: Look, all those commandments before and all those that follow are very important. But if you don't see the big picture, a fundamental overarching sense of the purpose of all these commandments, you've missed the very reasons why the Jewish people were given the Torah.

Some see this sentence as the source for the Jewish version of the concept of *Imitatio Dei,* which refers to the notion that as human beings we have an obligation to imitate or emulate God. Rabbi Seymour Siegel noted that there are several other sentences scattered throughout the Torah that are also seen as the possible sources for *Imitatio Dei.*[1] Siegel gives our sentence as a source for the concept, but also suggests six other sentences. Some of the other source-texts cited are rather particular to the observance of certain commandments (e.g. resting on the Sabbath, referencing Exod 20:10–11; loving the stranger, referencing Deut 10:18–19). Three in particular all have very similar language (Deut 10:12; 11:22 and 26:17), using the expression *lalechet [b'chol] dirachav,* to walk in [all] His ways. Talmudic commentaries stress that the attributes we are asked to emulate are ones of compassion, mercy, kindness, graciousness; to be hospitable, charitable, to clothe the naked and so on. We are not, however, called upon to emulate God's stern justice.

I am struck by a very fundamental difference between these latter verses as sources for *Imitatio Dei* and the one that I initially referenced. One could easily contend that the only way in which we can demonstrate our being holy as the penultimate expression of *Imitatio Dei* is through our behavior or actions. But I'd like to suggest that there is a different possible lesson to be learned from this important "speed bump" of "You shall be holy."

It would be possible to see the ethical and social behaviors addressed by the other "source verses" as ones that are noble general principles, not specifically bound to religion, much less a commanding and revelatory voice that we heard at Sinai and continues to speak to us through the generations. They are core statements of ways of interacting that engender a caring and nurturing society concerned about the welfare of its citizens. But they speak more to the greater utilitarian societal good than to a larger sense

1. Seymour Siegel, "Imitation of God." *Encyclopedia Judaica,* Vol.9, p.737–8.

of purpose and mission of who we are, what we do and what we aspire to become. "You shall be holy because I your God am holy" tells me that even if I don't see the value to me or to others, even if there is no apparent unmet need in the other who stands before me, there is always an unmet aspirational need, a higher calling that resides within me. That calling to be holy should drive us to consistently seek to be responsive to others in ways to emulate God. It is our mission to see ourselves as partners with God in making this world a better place.

Let me present a fascinating, specific example. Maimonides, in his *Mishneh Torah*, Laws of Gifts to the Poor,[2] lists a hierarchy of ways of being charitable. Reaching into my pocket to offer some money in response to a request from a poor person is fulfilling several positive commandments and also fulfilling several "negative" commandments as well, i.e. not making myself inured to the needs of the poor. Yet that is the lowest form of charity. The highest form of charity is entering into a business partnership with an individual, enabling that person to have dignity and providing a long-range solution to the unfortunate situation that he or she had been in. Both reflect ways to be cognizant of *Imitatio Dei*, but it is the highest form of charity that perhaps emanates from a broad sense of our need to be holy.

What is essential to both approaches is that we recognize that God created humanity *b'tzelem elokim,* in the image of God. That means that our obligation to be holy, to be God-like, requires us to look at all other human beings and to see that spark of God in them. The Midrash[3] tells us of a discussion between two of the classic rabbinic scholars, Rabbi Akiva and Ben Azzai, regarding what might be considered the single-most important principle articulated in the Torah. While Rabbi Akiva is well known for stating that the most important principle in the Torah is "And you shall love your friend as yourself" (Lev 19:18), the other, lesser known

---

2. Maimonides, *Mishneh Torah*, Ch.10, Sec. 7–14.

3. *Bereishit Rabbah*, 24:7. This Midrashic collection is among the earliest, 5th Century CE, and is comprised of both line-by-line commentary on the book of Genesis as well as parables, sayings and legal principles.

view expressed by Ben Azzai was: "This is the book of the generations of *Adam*. In the day of God's creating *Adam,* in the image
of God He created him." (Gen 5:1) If we start from the premise
that acknowledges and seeks to find that divine spark and image
in others, we will seek to make this world a better place for all its
inhabitants, as we strive to be holy, in *Imitatio Dei.*

14

INJUSTICES OF JUDGMENT, MEASUREMENT, WEIGHT AND QUANTITY

THE TORAH IS OFTEN viewed as a document in which less is more. Each word or phrase matters. We derive numerous legal decisions and moral lessons from interpretations arising out of exacting and precise statements, but also from those which appear vague or non-specific. In this vein, biblical commentators—both classic and modern—are sensitive to words, phrases and even whole sentences or commandments that on the surface seem unnecessary or redundant. Within the portion of *Kedoshim*, we encounter one such example.

> You shall not do an injustice in judgment, you should not be partial to a weak person, and you should not favor a big person. You shall judge your fellow with justice. (Lev 19:15)

Classic commentaries, such as Rashi, view this a referring to an actual judge, and detail the various terms that are used to describe a judge who violates this precept, as well as the long-term implications for the Jewish people if such types of judicial practice are commonplace. In an unusual repetition at the end of the same chapter in Leviticus, the Torah appears to restate what we just read, albeit slightly differently.

> You shall not do an injustice in judgment, in measurement, in weight, and in quantity. (Lev 19:25)

Rashi and others comment that if this is meant again to apply to a formal "judge," then it would be truly redundant. However, they explain that this seeming repetition refers to one who is doing business, conveying a sense that Judaism sets the same standards related to equity, fairness and honesty in individual business transactions as it does for judicial interactions.

But what more can we learn from this, and specifically what do we learn from the additive language, going beyond the injustice in judgment that appears in both verses to the additional terms found in verse 35, " . . .in measurement, in weight and in quantity?" It is often useful to examine the verse or verses that precede a commandment to see how they may relate to the commandment and our possible understanding of it. And in this instance the verses that precede both verse 15 and verse 35 can be instructive of a broader perspective on the ways in which we should conduct ourselves as Jews in our interactions with the rest of humanity.

Verse 15, our original commandment, is preceded by

> You shall not curse a deaf person, and you shall not place a stumbling block before a blind person. And you shall fear your God, I am the Lord. (verse 14)

We all stand as judges of the other and we are judged by the other as well, whether knowingly or unknowingly, consciously or unconsciously. Just prior to a moment of judgment, be it casual or formal, we are present with all of our positive and negative attributes, psychological dynamics, strengths and weakness that we possess, which define who we are at that moment in time. The Torah may be telling us here that we will inescapably make errors of judgment if we are mean-spirited, angry, hostile and cruel with regard to the other who is different from us. If we take Verse 14 in the most literal sense, we are describing someone who has a malicious disregard for the other who is more vulnerable, and a willful intent to do harm despite, or perhaps precisely because of, the other's inability to defend against this harm. And as the classic commentators therefore note, this type of behavior has implications that transcend the moment or interaction between the principals, for it lays a foundation that is destructive to the "judge," the "judged" and the national character of a people and its future.

Verse 34 gives us the broad picture of how to conduct ourselves.

> The alien who resides with you shall be to you like a citizen of yours and you shall love him/her as yourself, because you were aliens in the land of Egypt. I am the Lord, your God.

Rashi tells us that the lesson that we are to learn from our own experience of being strangers in the land of Egypt is that we should be sensitive to the experience of the alien or the immigrant and therefore be reluctant to be overly judgmental of the other. There is a sensitivity here that requires us to look inward, before we cast a judging eye outward. We need to reflect and think before we speak, to take seriously the short-term and long-term implications of our judgments, for they have implications for us, our families, our communities and the very welfare of our people and the world. And why is this all important? Simply because we are told in the opening line of this portion, "You shall be holy, because, I the Lord, your God, am holy." Admittedly the bar has been set high as an aspirational goal and we need to understand that we will always fall somewhere short of fully achieving that goal. It should, however, serve as a humbling reminder of the perils and abuses of judgment that can serve as stumbling blocks for each of us on our own spiritual journeys.

Verse 35 now provides us with the second" occurrence of our commandment, where in addition to the injustice of judgment, we are warned against injustices in " . . .measure, in weight and in quantity." Here we are given further details of the ways in which we can have a distorted or even perverse view of our fellow human being. When we judge someone, is it based on really knowing them as an individual, who they are as a complex person, no less complex than we are ourselves even if they are "different" than us? What do we truly know about how this person thinks, feels, understands, experiences before we "pronounce our judgment?" Are we certain that in our taking the "measure of the person" that we have not mistakenly characterized the other due to his/her being different from us, perhaps reflecting a worldview that we don't understand, or don't care to understand? How do we weigh the words, concepts, ideas and feelings of others? Is everything other than what we think, feel or believe inherently less worthy, less "weighty," less meaningful, less possible, less true? And do we minimize someone else's views and the worthiness of those views because we believe we have "strength in numbers," i.e. that more people agree with our perspective and therefore "might makes right?" One might reflect upon the classic Talmudic principle with regard to the testimony of witnesses, "two is like one hundred," to realize that our rabbis understood the dangers of believing that we are more right simply because the "numbers are on our side."

SECTION IV

ON THE ROAD: THE DESERT JOURNALS

15

WHY COUNT, WHO COUNTS, WHAT REALLY COUNTS?

WHILE THE FOURTH BOOK of the Torah is called *Bamidbar* in the original Hebrew, which means "in the wilderness," in English it is referred to as the "Book of Numbers." This is because the opening passages tell of a census of the Children of Israel, the third such census within one year of the exodus from Egypt.

> And God spoke to Moses in the wilderness of Sinai in the tent of assembly on the first day of the second month of the second year of their departure from the land of Egypt, saying. *Siu* (Hebrew for "count" or more literally "lift up") the heads of all the congregations of the children of Israel according to their families; according to their ancestors' houses, with the number of the names, all the males by their *gulgolotom* (Hebrew for "by their skulls" understood to mean each according to their half-shekel, a specific silver weight, donation per person.) (Num 1:1–2)

Three important broad questions emerge for me: Why Count?; Who Counts?; And What Counts?

WHY COUNT?

Certainly the most basic reasons for counting something are to know the extent of what you have, to be able to assess what the value of that is, and to exercise and maintain control over it. Of course that is an anthropocentric perspective. But what of God's counting of the Jewish people or commanding that we be counted? Of what purpose or function is it to God? Rabbi Jonathan Sacks, the former Chief Rabbi of the United Kingdom, suggests that we are given two very disparate reasons for counting.[1] On the one hand, Rashi, commenting on this opening passage to the Book of Numbers, suggests that God counts the Jewish people because they are so dear and precious; in effect, this is a sign of God's love. Yet Sacks also notes that in an earlier passage in Exodus, it is clear that counting is fraught with risk

> And God spoke to Moses saying. When you count the heads of the children of Israel according to their counts, each of them shall give a ransom of their souls to God when they are being counted, and there shall not be a plague among them in the counting of them. (Exod 30:11–12)

So the act of counting can serve as a means to demonstrate love of the other, as well as a way to demand of the other commitment, responsibility and accountability.

Sacks and many others also note that the choice of the word "*siu*" to lift up, as opposed to several other alternative words in Hebrew for counting, bespeaks the ways in which God is commanding us to use the act of counting as a means to elevate the individual being counted. However, it is not my act of counting that invests value in you. Rather, I am counting you because you have an inherent value, and I wish to communicate my awareness and acknowledgement of that to you. Sacks also makes reference to a lesser-known blessing, mentioned in the Talmud (*Berachot* 58a), which is to be recited upon seeing 600,000 Israelites in one place: "Blessed are you, God, Our Lord, ruler of the universe, who

---

1. *Covenant & Conversation* (Bamidbar, 24 May 2014/24 Iyar 5774)

discerns secrets." Sacks interprets this to mean that it is ultimately only God who has the capability to recognize each of our unique qualities and attributes and to truly see each of us as individuals, even in a crowd of 600,000, much less in a world of more than 7.2 billion people.

WHO COUNTS?

Who counts in this opening to the Book of Numbers, and who counts in a variety of settings and for a variety of purposes in the Torah and in later traditional texts presents more difficulties. The simplest and most succinct answer, albeit painful to this author, is males. Whether you retain and celebrate those gender-based differences, transform the traditions to find new ways to have more egalitarian approaches within the framework of Jewish traditions, or choose to completely eliminate these differences, is not the subject of this chapter. But even within a male-dominated, gender-based system, it is worthwhile to note that historically Judaism is replete with a wide range of "cohorts of significance" in which the number of males that are required for something "to count" varies. And once the necessary numbers constitute the particular cohort of significance for the intended purpose, adding more numbers of people for the same purpose does not make that larger cohort any better, or of greater value. Several examples should suffice.

In the area of giving testimony, there are certain circumstances where one individual's testimony is considered sufficient for an official judgment to be made. An example is regarding testimony that a woman's husband was killed or died [in a war] and thus she can be considered a widow and free to remarry.[2] Hence, only one witness is required.

In general, however, in testimony, we require two witnesses. But once we have the two witnesses who are deemed appropriate for the role and testimony they are giving, they are necessary and

---

2. Talmud, *Ketubot*, 22b-23a.

sufficient. In fact, they are considered to be as authoritative as if we have one hundred people offering the same testimony.[3]

For a prayer quorum, a *minyan*, ten adults are required, which then allows the Torah to be read in the formal public Torah readings, as well as for certain prayers to be said. Eleven or eleven hundred is not any better or more valuable than the minimum required ten.[4]

The formal sanctification of God's name in public, classically referred to as *Kiddush HaShem* or martyrdom, was seen as requiring a quorum of ten. And, similar to the prayer quorum referenced above, adding numbers to the group does not in any way add to the holiness of the act or make it more valuable to God.[5]

Traditional Judaism has distinctions of significance between the private and public domain as it relates to carrying objects on the Sabbath. Many Modern Orthodox communities go to great pains, legally and financially, to construct an *eruv*, creating a physical vehicle that symbolically encloses a public space as well as symbolically unifies the community and transforms the space from public to private vis a vis carrying on the Sabbath. However, there are areas that are rabbinically defined as forever public because more than 600,000 people can be found in them at any given time and are thus deemed to be unable to be transformed from public to private space as per the above *eruv* approach.[6]

The question that we need to ask is what these various examples all mean about our question of "who counts." I am less concerned, however intellectually interesting it may be, as to why these specific situations require the different numbers they do. My focus is on the broader lesson to be derived. We certainly can extract several themes of importance.

The first, and perhaps most important, is that numbers both matter and don't matter at all. Or more precisely, numbers matter

---

3. *Hilchot Edut* 18:3 of Maimonides, as cited in Lorberbaum, p.117.

4. Based on several biblical sources, including Num. 14:2–7. See also Talmud *Megillah* 23b.

5. Talmud *Megillah* 23b.

6. Talmud *Shabbat,* 6b.

for certain things and situations and not for others. Sometimes 600,000 is a big and important number and can impact on the lives and behavior of individuals, or hundreds, or thousands or millions of others. And sometimes there is remarkable and comparable power that resides even within one individual, whose testimony might prohibit something to individuals, or hundreds, or thousands, or millions. Also, think of the famed Talmudic statement in the Tractate of Sanhedrin 37a, "If someone saves an individual life, it is as if an entire world was saved."

The second lesson to be derived is that at times when certain numbers matter, once you have achieved that requisite number and the status has been invested in the group, more is not better, bigger is not better. It speaks to the value of a group that represents significance. It is a lesson regarding perspective and concomitant humility in pursuing one's mission and purpose.

WHAT REALLY COUNTS?

It is possible to look at the Hebrew titles of each of the five books of the Torah and each of their themes in order to gain some perspective on the issue of what really counts. *Bereisheet*, Genesis literally means "In the beginning," in which we are focused on individuals, the first man and woman and then eventually the patriarchs and matriarchs, with detailed listings of their various offspring. Who the eventual "seventy" souls are that go down and settle in the land of Egypt as the book of Genesis draws to a close is important. *Shemot*, Exodus—literally "Names." Here we experience the transition from the individual to the larger group and thus we speak of the 600,000 that God eventually takes out of Egypt (a figure based on males of a certain age, the actual total number of people being certainly well in excess of 1.5 million). *Vayikra*, Leviticus—literally "And He [God] called," brings us to a critical point. What you are being called upon to do and to become will be more important than the names of individuals or the total numbers of individuals. *Bamidbar*, ironically translated as Numbers, but literally means "In the wilderness." It hints that even as we are called upon to act in certain ways and to aspire to be a holy nation, an *am kadosh*, the journey, the willingness to approach the unknown in a state of openness, is critical in shaping us to who and what we will become. And *Devarim*, Deuteronomy, literally "things" or "words." It may tell us that perhaps we are all only valuable and worthy of being counted if we understand that the relationship between the words we speak and the things we do reflects our true value as individuals and as a nation.

The *Haftorah*, the words from the Prophets that are read after the conclusion of the Torah reading on the Sabbath and festivals, for this portion of *Bamidbar*, is taken from the prophet Hosea. The opening lines speak to the issue of the counting of the Jewish people:

> And it will be that the number of the Children of Israel will be like the sand of the ocean, which cannot be measured and cannot be counted . . . (Hos 2:1)

Yet we know that this has never described the population of the Jewish people historically. In current times we comprise a minuscule percentage of the world's population. So the issue again becomes one of perspective as to what really counts if it is in fact not "numbers." For this we need to look at the closing sentences of this prophetic reading, where Hosea speaks on behalf of God to the Jewish people.

> And I will betroth you unto Me for eternity; and I will betroth you unto Me in righteousness and judgment, and loving-kindness and mercy; and I will betroth you unto Me in faithfulness and you shall know God. (Hos 1:21–22)

There are times that counting is important and absolute numbers count. However, bigger is not better. Achieving a certain critical mass to comprise a group that has value, purpose and mission may be at times essential. In order to be engaged in a profound committed relationship with God that really counts, however, we will be measured by our demonstration of the values of righteousness, fairness, loving-kindness, and mercy. A pre-condition for that is our acknowledgment that what counts first and foremost about any individual is that he or she was created *b'tzelem Elohim*, in the image of God. It is the great equalizer that preemptively defines the inherent value of each individual and that defines on the most foundational level what really counts. Then, and only then, are we capable of being a faithful people of faith, worthy of knowledge of God.

16

WE SEARCH FOR GOD WHO SEARCHES FOR US

I SUSPECT THAT EVERYONE has at least one personal story of a missed opportunity in life that leaves you with a profound sense of regret and a desire to have a second chance to fulfill that opportunity. Whether as banal as a missed swing at bat that precluded the game-winning run being scored, or a missed opportunity that led to a forever lost love, it is an unpleasant feeling that we may know too well.

In the third portion read in the book of Numbers, entitled *Behaaloticha,* Chapter 9 opens with a recounting of the observance of the Festival of Passover by the Jewish people in the second year following the exodus from Egypt. At the appointed time on the appointed day, the 14th of the month of *Nissan,* we are told that they fully observed, in accordance with all the statues and laws, bringing of the paschal sacrifice. A remarkable story is then told.

> And there were people who had been ritually impure [as a result of exposure to a corpse] and [therefore] had been unable to do the paschal sacrifice on that day, and they came before Moses and before Aaron on that day. And these people said, We are ritually impure as a result of exposure to a corpse; why should we be precluded [or a variant translation of the Hebrew *negara*: "we be subtracted"]

from bringing the sacrifice of God at its appointed time
from among the children of Israel? (Num 9:6–13)

One of the striking things here is that this is the first and only
example in which a group of people are raising the issue of missed
opportunities and a desire to have a second chance. In the entire
balance of the Torah, we don't find any stories of someone saying
that he or she should be afforded an opportunity to have an official
"make-up date" that will enable them to fulfill a missed responsibility. Moreover, given the extreme significance of observance of
the Passover festival and the offering of the paschal sacrifice with
the accompanying family meal—what we now call the Passover
Seder—on its appointed historical date, it would appear that any
"make-up date" would be sorely lacking in its symbolic connec-
tions to the original sacrifice, meal and the exodus experience.

Rather remarkably, Moses' reply is to tell them to wait while
he, in turn, waits to hear what God will command them to do.
God's subsequent reply and new commandment to Moses is startling in its responsiveness to the request.

> And God spoke to Moses saying. "Speak to the children
> of Israel and say. If any person is ritually impure [due
> to exposure to a corpse] or on a faraway road/journey
> from you, or in future generations, they shall do the
> paschal sacrifice for God. On the second month [i.e.
> Iyar, the month which follows Nissan] on the fourteenth
> day between the two evenings, they shall do the paschal
> sacrifice and with matzot and bitter herbs they shall eat
> it. They shall not leave any of the sacrifice over for the
> morning nor shall they break any bones; according to all
> the statutes of the paschal sacrifice they shall perform it.
> [But] the person who is ritually pure and has not been
> on a faraway journey [i.e. has no excuse not to perform
> the paschal sacrifice on the originally appointed day] and
> has failed to do the sacrifice, is cut off from his people, for
> he has not brought the sacrifice of God in its appointed
> time; it is his sin and he shall bear it. (Num 9–13)

Not only are they granted an official alterative Passover ob-
servance/paschal sacrifice date, which we refer to as *Pesach Sheini,*

literally the "Second Passover," but God extends this opportunity through an amplification of additional circumstances under which one could avail him/herself of this alternative date that was not even raised by this initial group of supplicants nor by Moses. Now, those who are away on a journey that has them far from their family/people on the fourteenth day of *Nissan*, can also celebrate *Pesach Sheini*.

It is difficult to understand what has transpired here. The commanding God who doesn't offer alternatives to missed opportunities for other ritual observances appears to accede to the impassioned wishes of a group seeking to observe the Paschal sacrifice. Furthermore, this is not a one-time commandment. God makes this permanent for all generations and goes beyond the wishes of this group and adds a set of circumstances that would seem in fact to be preventable, i.e. don't embark on a journey to a faraway place for several weeks before the fourteenth of the month of Nissan.

There is a remarkably similar story, not one of a missed opportunity in the pure sense as in our case here of *Pesach Sheini*, but a later example of what appears to be a remarkably and uncharacteristically responsive God to the wishes of a sincere and impassioned group, with some parallels of language to our section above. Later in the book of Numbers, we are told of the five daughters of Zelaphchad, who present themselves to Moses, Elazar the priest, the chiefs of the tribes and the entire congregation, with the following statement and request.

> Our father died in the wilderness and he was not among the congregation that gathered against God within the congregation of Korach, for he died of his own sin, and he did not have any sons. Why should the name of our father be precluded [or a variant translation of the Hebrew yigara "be subtracted"] from amidst his family because he didn't have a son [which would, as of this point in the Torah appear be the law that the daughters wouldn't inherit his territorial/familial holdings in the land of Israel]? Give us a possession among our father's brothers. (Num 27:3–5)

Moses proceeds to bring this request before God, who again remarkably states that the daughters of Zelaphchad are correct, articulating in several sentences a new law regarding the ability of a daughter to inherit in the absence of a son. This is stated as a law for all generations, as opposed to an exception specific for, and unique to, the daughters of Zelaphchad.

The difference between the group of people who were ritually unable to bring the paschal sacrifice and the daughters of Zelaphchad has not escaped me. The fundamental parallel however, amplified by the similar use of the Hebrew word [*nigara*, "we should be subtracted" and *yigara*, "it shall be subtracted"] is significant. In both cases, defying what appears to be the stated law which offers no alternatives or flexibility, impassioned sincere groups contend that applying God's law, in effect, would not be just nor moral. And God accedes in both instances. What are we to make of this and what message does it have for us?

I think the answer requires us to look back to the portion of *Behaaloticha* in the book of Numbers. In order to cope with the increasing burden of responsibility of dealing with the people's spiritual needs, Moses gathers seventy leaders from among the tribes who will serve as the elders. God's spirit descends upon these seventy leaders, such that we are told:

> . . .and He gave [His spirit] on the seventy men, the elders, and it was when the spirit rested upon them they prophesied, and then they did not continue [i.e. to have prophecy, and appear to then leave the area in which they had gathered]. (Num 11:25)

However, what ensues is that two men, Eldad and Medad, who were among the original seventy, did continue to have these prophetic abilities. Joshua, Moses' heir apparent to-be, is shocked by their behavior and runs to inform Moses, suggesting that they should be restrained and detained for punishment. But Moses' reply is to the contrary:

> And Moses said to him [Joshua]: "Are you jealous on my behalf? And who would make it so that all of the nation

of God would be prophets because God would give his spirit on them." (Num 11:29).

Moses' response is striking for its humility and for his modeling of leadership that is less self-absorbed and more focused on the ultimate, larger goal. The idea that the Jewish people might be better off, that our religious and spiritual life as a people of faith would be enhanced if there were even more people willing to invoke a sense of the divine spirit, is an extraordinary one. Moses understands that not only does this NOT undermine his leadership, it also doesn't undermine God's law or will.

Abraham Joshua Heschel wrote two books looking at the quest for spirituality and an intimate relationship with God, viewed from two different perspectives, *Man's Quest for God* and *God in Search of Man*. In the stories of *Pesach Sheini* and the Daughters of Zelaphchad, the disaffected individuals who suggest that God's laws do not sufficiently address their particular situation first raise their issues by approaching Moses—and in effect God—with a request framed within a spirit of spiritual yearning. These aren't challenges to leadership. Rather, they are spiritual engagements of the most profound nature. They say to God: You have given us a Torah and a foundation. Let us continue that revelatory process for us and for the generations to come. And they are rewarded by a responsive God. We might wonder whether the challenge that was placed before us at Sinai was to be so engaged in the religious process that we too become that man or woman in search of the God who sits waiting in search of us.

17

WHEN OUR ANGER AND JEALOUSY CONSUMES US

LIFE WAS NOT EASY for Moses. His very mettle as a leader was tested, from the moment he begrudgingly accepted God's command to return to his people in Egypt to help free them through the course of the forty years of wandering in the desert. Perhaps the most famous and direct assault on his role, credibility and very God-given authority came from Korach, first cousin to Moses, Aaron and Miriam.

> And Korach, son of Izhar, son of Kohath, son of Levi, and Dathan and Abiram, sons of Eliab and On, son of Peleth, sons of Reuben took and got up in front of Moses, and two hundred and fifty people from the children of Israel, chieftains of the congregation, prominent ones of the assembly, people of repute. And they assembled against Moses and against Aaron and said to them: You have too much! Because all of the congregation, all of them are holy and God is among them. And why do you raise yourselves up over God's community? And Moses listened and fell on his face. And he spoke to Korach and to all the congregation saying: In the morning God will make known who is His and who is holy and He will bring him close to Him. And He will bring the one he chooses close to Him. (Num 16:1–5)

The Midrash gives several examples of what the rabbis imagined to be Korach's pseudo-religious challenges to Moses' interpretations of God's law. One of these examples related to the commandment of putting fringes (*tzitzit*) on the corner of a four cornered garment. The commandment regarding the fringes, where we are told " . . .and they shall put a blue string on the fringe in the corner"(Num 15:38) appears just sentences before Korach's rebellion. Korach had the 250 leaders dressed entirely in wool garments that had been dyed completely in blue, and asked Moses if this would satisfy the commandment, to which Moses replied "No." Korach mocked him saying, "The entire garment dyed in blue would not suffice while merely dying four strings would?" The second apparent challenge pertained to the commandment to put a mezuzah on the doorposts of one's house. Korach asked Moses "If a house is filled with books of the Torah does it still require the placement of a mezuzah on its doorposts?" to which Moses replied "Yes." Again, scoffing, Korach retorted and said, "All the words of the Torah in the house are not sufficient but having just a few sentences of them on a parchment on the doorposts does suffice?"[1]

Did Korach expect Moses and Aaron to shrink away and turn over their power to him? Did Korach actually believe that Moses and Aaron were either acting of their own accord or had significantly overstepped the limits of their God-given position? And if the latter, did Korach view God as powerless to put Moses and Aaron back in their place or indifferent to their exceeding the bounds of their authority? We are led to understand by the Rabbis that these challenges were really smokescreens, attempts to make Moses look foolish, and not well-intentioned reasoned questions reflecting a variant understanding of the actual commandments. The outcome of Korach's challenge is a public display of Korach's sinfulness and Moses' rectitude, ending with the earth opening its mouth and swallowing up Korach, his family and his followers.

---

1. Midrah *Bamidbar Rabbah*, 18. This Midrashic collection is comprised of material compiled in the medieval period, as well as material which may have existed as early as the 4th Century CE.

The story of Korach may well be a relatively simple story of a man, who despite his lineage and position, nonetheless falls prey to his overwhelming, blinding jealousy. This then distorts his perceptions of Moses and Aaron, impairs his own judgment, and creates a dangerous level of risk-taking in which he was willing to sacrifice not only himself, but others as well in the process. But we need to ask ourselves what lessons we might learn from this concerning the appropriate circumstance and approaches in which to challenge others.

It may be useful to look at the two commandments previously referenced in the pseudo-legalistic challenges to Moses' and Aaron's authority. The wearing of a four cornered garment with four blue fringes could well be something that is not necessarily apparent to others, and thus relates to the personal domain. But the placement of a *mezuzah* on the doorpost of our homes is very much within the public domain, visible to all who see the outside of our homes, and visible to all who enter into our homes. These two spheres may stand as metaphors for what we do when we attack another person. We often tend to attack the "interior" of a person, calling to question their character, their intentions, their credibility and their integrity. We also can attack their more public side, i.e. their appearance, positions or opinions. We can mock them, as if to say that everyone else also shares our views.

In reviewing our text, I am struck by Moses' minimalism in his response to criticism. Rather than striking back aggressively, appropriately citing his "credentials" as being God's emissary who redeemed the people from Egypt and received the Torah on Sinai, or replying with fiery indignation at even being questioned, Moses is understated and humble in his response to Korach. The most we see in the way of an emotional and passionate response concerns the critique of his brother Aaron. Here, rather than chastising Korach for criticizing him, Moses says "And Aaron, what is he that you complain against him?" (Num 16:11) Moses' overall response is to, in effect say: It is not up to me to say who represents God. It is God who will show that. We have in this story a hint of the ways in which we should proceed with caution when we assume that we are speaking on behalf of God as we chastise or criticize others. It is far too easy to be swept up in the moment and the passion of our convictions and beliefs and be so certain that we are in the right, and others are simply wrong. While casting aspersions on the motives of others, our own less-than-noble purposes are driving us in dangerous directions, with consequences that may far exceed that which we are able to realize at the moment in which we lead with our mouths and not our minds.

And is there something special that we should additionally learn from the most unusual punishment that Korach and his followers received? They were swallowed alive by the earth. Is there any more poignant way to remind us all of our commonality, of the great equalizer, that we are all descendants of that very first, and flawed, Adam? This is the very same Adam who demonstrated a difficulty in accepting responsibility for his own shortcomings but so easily blamed someone else. Thus, in the earth consuming Korach we see that we can, ourselves, be consumed by our own anger or jealousy that has led us to seek to demolish the other.

I am left with a question as to whether there are times when in fact arguments are for "the sake of heaven." What do I think the story of Korach teaches us? Before we proceed to open our mouth with the argument that we are so certain is truly for the sake of heaven, Wait. Pause. Think. And ask yourself, and perhaps ask someone else, whether your motives are as pure and as noble as you think they are. Think about what you are going to say, how you are going to say it, and whether your goal is to give feedback or to mock and or demolish the other with whom you disagree. And before you proceed, remember that even when we "win" an argument, perhaps a degree of humility is appropriate.

There is a famous Midrash cited in the Talmud (*Megilah*, 10b) that God did not let the angels sing a joyous song at the drowning of the Egyptians in the Red Sea following the Jewish people's miraculous walk through the very same waters. In this classic version of the Midrash, God tells the angels that the Egyptians are also the works of His hands and it would be inappropriate to rejoice over their deaths, however deserved. Aviva Gottlieb Zornberg, noted biblical scholar, cites a lesser known variation of this Midrash,[2] in which the angels are commanded to refrain from celebrating because they see the anguish of the *Jewish people* all night long. And what was this anguish? Citing a variety of sources, Zornberg weaves a picture of the Jewish people being terrorized because their fate was still being determined in the night prior to their redemption. It was not clear cut that they were worthy of being saved, and this awareness left them in a state of terror.[3] We need to understand that we are more similar than dissimilar to our fellow human beings. It is difficult at times to know which one of us is "right" and which one is "wrong." Even in an argument allegedly for the sake of heaven, there are no clear "winners" and "losers." And perhaps we should all tremble in advance because in some way the "works of God's hands" may be harmed in the process.

---

2. *The Particulars of Rapture*, p. 42, citing *Pirkei D Rabbi Eliezer.*

3. Zornberg, ibid, p.215, citing *Pirkei D'Rabbi Eliezer*,42.

18

HOW CAN I CURSE THAT WHICH GOD DOES NOT CURSE

AN ENTIRE TORAH PORTION, called *Balak*, in the book of Numbers, tells us about how the non-Jewish prophet Bilaam is engaged by Balak, King of Moab, to assist him in his attempts to conquer the traveling Jewish people, by cursing them. The very opening passage of this portion states, "And Balak the son of Zippor saw all that Israel did to the Amorites (Num. 22:1). Bilaam, whom classic Rabbinic sources see as a prophet of very high abilities, initially reflects his ambivalence by telling Balak's messengers that he needs them to stay the night while he consults with God as to whether he should accept their offer and go ahead and curse the Jewish people. God's response is rather clear:

> And God said to Bilaam, "Don't go with them and don't curse the nation [the Jewish people], for it is blessed. (Num 22:12)

A clear message, seemingly recognized and understood by Bilaam to be coming directly from God, compels Bilaam to send Balak's messengers back to Balak the next morning, not having completed their mission. But Balak still seeks Bilaam's support and sends even more prestigious emissaries to solicit his assistance. Bilaam refuses again despite all the offers of monetary compensation, invoking his inability to do something that would be contrary to God's wishes. And yet that night God suggests to Bilaam that he should go with Balak's messengers but to say only that which God will bid him to say. Perhaps a tad too overzealous, the next morning Bilaam arises and saddles up his own donkey and starts out on the journey. We then are told:

> And Bilaam arose in the morning and he saddled his donkey and he went with the princes of Moab. And God was angry because he went, and angel of God was positioned on the path in order to be an obstacle to him, and he rode on his donkey and his two lads were with him. And the donkey saw the angel of God positioned on the path and his sword was outstretched in his hand; and the donkey veered from the path and went into the field, and Bilaam struck the donkey in order to turn her onto the path. And the angel of God stood in the path of the vineyards, a boundary/fence on this [side] and a boundary/fence on this [side]. And the donkey saw the angel of God, and she was pressed to the wall, and she pressed Bilaam's foot to the wall, and he continued to hit her [the donkey]. And the angel of God continued passing and it stood in a narrow place such that there was no room [for the donkey] to turn to the right or to the left. And the donkey saw the angel of God, and she sat down under Bilaam, and Bilaam was angry and he struck the donkey with his staff. And God opened up the mouth of the donkey and she said to Bilaam, What have I done to you such that you have struck me, these three times? And Bilaam said to the donkey, Because you have abused me, if I had only had my sword in my hand I would have now slaughtered you. And the donkey said to Bilaam, Am I not your donkey, [the one that] you have ridden on me from your beginnings until now? Have I typically done this to you? And he [Bilaam] said, No. And God uncovered Bilaam's eyes and he saw the angel of God positioned on the path and his sword drawn and he knelt and he prostrated himself to his face. And the angel of God said to him [Bilaam], For what do you hit your donkey these three times? Behold I went out to be an obstacle, because the path was dangerous because of

me. And the donkey saw me and she turned from me
this three times. Perhaps if she had not turned, now—
certainly—you I would have killed and I would have let
the donkey live. And Bilaam said to the angel of God, I
have sinned, for I did not know that you were positioned
to confront me on the path, and now if this is evil in your
eyes, I will return. (Num 22:1–35)

Again, Bilaam is told to continue on his journey, but to say
only that which God will tell him. Bilaam eventually arrives at
Moab and tells Balak to have seven altars built for him, to have
seven male bulls and seven rams gathered so he could offer one of
each on each of the seven altars, after which he will then communicate to Balak that which God tells him. After doing this, Bilaam
utters the first of a series of poetic statements about the Jewish
people, statements of praise, much to the consternation and exas-
peration of Balak

> How can I curse that which God has not cursed, and
> how can I denounce that which God has not denounced?
> (Num 23:8)

In the second series of poetic utterances in praise of Israel,
which follows in verses 18–24, Bilaam states that he was taken
there [by God] to bless [the people] and God blessed them and
he, Bilaam cannot, retract this. Continuing this theme he explains
that:

> God did not find fault in Jacob and didn't see a burden in
> Israel. (Num 23:21)

And later in the third in the series of blessings,

> The word of Bilaam, the son of Beor and the word of the
> man, opened eye (Hebrew: *sh'tum ha'ayin*). Word of the
> one who hears God's utterances and who sees God's vi-
> sions, falling but with eyes uncovered. (Num 24:3–4)

While most commentators, classic and modern, do translate
shtum ha'ayin as "opened eye," there are two Talmudic sources
(*Sanhedrin*, 105a and *Nidah*, 31a) which translate the phrase in the

direct opposite way, i.e. "closed-eyed." We'll return to these seemingly incompatible translations later when we discuss Bilaam and his talking donkey.

Bilaam then utters one of the most famous sentences describing the Jewish people, one that begins the first part of traditional, daily morning prayer service, the *Psukei D'zimra*. Upon entering the synagogue for the morning prayers, we are enjoined to say Bilaam's very words:

> How goodly are your tents, Jacob, your dwelling places,
> Israel. (Num 24:5)

Thus, Bilaam has been truly transformed. He has "seen the light" and is now able to praise and bless the Jewish people.

We need to ask ourselves what has occurred here in this entire story in which vision is invoked repeatedly. We have a talking, God-fearing donkey who sees better than his master who is a prophet and seer, and we have to question how someone can be both sharp-eyed and lacking in clarity of vision simultaneously.

In order to address these issues, let us examine the similarities and differences between our talking donkey and the first and only other animal in the Torah who speaks, the snake in the Garden of Eden. In the story of the snake and Eve and Adam described in Genesis we read:

> And the snake was slyer than all the other animals of the
> field that God made . . . (Gen 3:1)

This introductory fact about the God-given character of the snake serves to lay the groundwork for understanding how Eve could have been so easily duped to eat the fruit of the forbidden tree and in turn give it to Adam, who also ate some of the fruit. Eve and Adam are swayed by a highly independent, smooth-talking snake with a seductive message that tempts them with the potential to be equal to God.

Bilaam, the great prophet, with incredible clarity of vision, was unable to even see what path to choose. Whether blinded by his own internal arrogance and complacency that he always would have clear "vision," or blinded by the appeal to his ego, he falls far below the cognitive, perceptual and moral level of his own donkey. His donkey is an animal whose function is to be of service to others, but about which we learn nothing of its predisposed moral character or personality.

What the two animals clearly do share in common is that they can independently initiate, at their will, conversations with human beings. They are cogent, cognizant, interactive, strategic and convincing in their communications. They have sophisticated and nuanced insight into human beings, surpassing those human beings' abilities, at least for these remarkable two events. They function within the realm of moral/immoral or good/bad, the snake having a bad/immoral intention and the donkey having a good/moral intention. And finally, after their respective, rather startling and significant speaking roles, neither they nor any of their species nor any other animal speak again in the Torah. So we must ask ourselves what is the larger message that we human beings, endowed with intellectual, psychological and ethical/moral capabilities, are to learn from the "sinful" behavior of the snake and from the "righteous" behavior of the donkey? How does Bilaam, simultaneously sharp-eyed and impaired of vison, serve as a role model for us as we view our fellow human beings?

If we contrast the snake and the donkey, we may derive a lesson that regardless of what is a predisposed trait, we are expected to behave in certain moral and righteous ways. God demands such behavior from us and holds us accountable for failing to act in good, moral and righteous ways. We all bring predisposing variables to situations of moral choice. They are both the very fabric of our collective humanity and of our incredibly individual and unique personalities. In each of us there is perhaps both the Snake and the Donkey. Our task is to acknowledge those different and differing aspects of ourselves and to figure out how to see the righteous path and to walk on it.

In the classic novella, *The Little Prince* (1943) by Antoine de Saint Exupéry, the Fox, in saying goodbye to the Prince says:

Here is my secret. It is very simple: It is only with the
heart that one can see rightly; what is essential is invisible
to the eye.[1]

Perhaps our task begins with understanding precisely this
message, that we cannot rely upon what we are certain is our perception of fact, truth or reality. We need to guard against a tenden-
cy for extremist thinking and arrogance that assumes that we are
Godlike or that we alone are necessary and sufficient to know "the
Truth." At the very least, we need to pause and reflect and recon-
sider what we think we have seen, what we believe we understand
and what we are certain that we know, before we open our mouths
to speak to, with, and about another person. Bilaam's experience,
which causes his every attempt to curse the people to turn into a
blessing, isn't about looking at a different "thing" than what you
had looked at previously. Rather, it is about seeing something or
someone that you have viewed before, differently, through a different lens, without the adverse, vision-impairing filters which we
often bring to these opportunities.

The chapter's title is drawn from a previously cited verse:

How can I curse that which God has not cursed, and
how can I denounce that which God has not denounced?
(Num 23:8)

I too cannot curse that which God has not cursed. I need to
start out understanding my own limitations and the factors that
contribute to both my individual impaired vision and to my clarity of vision. I need to remember that even if it is not apparent to
me at that moment, I must always view the other person as an
equal who also was created b'tzelem Elohim, in the image of God.
Perhaps then we will find and create more opportunities to offer
blessings and words of kindness and praise.

---

1. Saint Exupery, p.63.

19

PINCHAS NEEDS A COVENANT OF PEACE AND A COVENANT OF PRIESTHOOD

CHAPTER 25 OF THE book of Numbers, encompassing the very end of the Torah portion of *Balak* and the opening passages of the portion of *Pinchas*, describes how the Jewish people (i.e. the men) veer from the path that God has given to them, through their sexual involvement with the daughters of Moab. This leads to their association with, and worship of, the gods of Moab, and specifically to the god, *Baal Peor*. This incurs the wrath of God articulated clearly to Moses. In response, Moses calls out to the Judges of Israel and commands them to kill all those people who have associated themselves with this foreign god. The Torah then continues with the account of a prominent Jewish man, *Zimri* the son of *Salu*, who brazenly "brings" (interpreted differently by classical commentators as: with the intention of marriage; with the intention of committing a sexual act; or, that he actually engaged in a sexual act) a Midianite woman, *Cozbi*, daughter of *Zur*, to a prominent place within the encampment before all the people and before Moses. This occurred while they were all mourning for Aaron, still within the thirty-days of mourning that were proscribed as a communal response to Aaron's death. It took place opposite the *Ohel Moed*, the Tent of Meeting. According to Rashi, Zimri inquires of

Moses whether he is permitted to be involved sexually with the woman. If it is forbidden, he wonders, what was the legal basis by which Moses had been permitted to marry Zipporah, the daughter of Jethro the high priest of Midian? Remarkably, Rashi further tells us that Moses had forgotten the law. Along comes Pinchas the son of Elazar, the son of Aaron, the priest. He takes a spear and impales both the man (Zimri) and the woman (Cozbi) together, enacting the very law that Moses had forgotten. According to Rashi, Pinchas was fulfilling the precept, *Kanain pogi'in bo*, the jealous ones shall kill him. Following this, something astonishing happens.

> And God spoke to Moses saying, Pinchas, the son of Elazar, the son of Aaron the priest, has brought back my fury from the children of Israel by his carrying out my jealousy among them, so I didn't destroy the children of Israel in my jealousy of them. Therefore, say: Here I am giving him my covenant of peace, and it shall be his and his seed's after him, a covenant of eternal priesthood because he was jealous for God, and he made atonement for the children of Israel. (Num 25:10–13)

Pinchas seems to be effectuating an outcome that appears to be consistent with God's command to Moses that the perpetrators of sexually promiscuous acts intertwined with idolatrous behavior should be killed. However we understand it, Pinchas' action seems to have calmed God's anger and mitigated against the possibility of God destroying the entire children of Israel. But if Pinchas was implementing the correct form of mandated punishment for an egregious offense, it isn't clear why he deserved some special reward. And his reward was a covenant, but was it a covenant of peace as is stated in verse 12, or was it a covenant of eternal priesthood as is stated in verse 13, or perhaps both?

We need to begin by looking at the notion of a covenant. Certainly the Torah is replete with various examples of covenants. Some entered into between two individuals while others are examples of covenants between God and a biblical figure, as is the case in our story regarding Pinchas. There is a striking difference between covenants between two people and covenants between God and an individual or a nation for that matter. A covenant entered into by two people, even if the circumstances that bring the two together involve some power dynamic, essentially involves a consensual relationship of two co-equals. Terms of the covenant are set and it may be fairly easy to identify when one of the parties violates the terms. If both parties are not satisfied with the outcome, the covenant no longer exists. While we can contend that individuals in the Bible, such as Pinchas, have demonstrated their commitment to a relationship with God such that they are consenting parties, this type of covenant is clearly a relationship of non-equals. It is initiated by God and the terms and conditions are defined by God as well. God proclaims that a covenant is being given to Pinchas, but we don't read of Pinchas' response. Nothing like: Thanks God, sounds appealing. Let me review the details with my attorney and my people will get back to your people if it's a deal. Pinchas is given, whether or not he likes it, wants it, or believes he needs it, a covenant, one so binding that it is not only for him but for all his descendants for all eternity. And the covenant itself? First in verse 12 it is a covenant of peace. An odd choice if Pinchas was simply implementing the appropriate punishment for the two sinners. What was the state of war or strife that Pinchas was in for which he needed peace – or was it merely for implementing this violent act itself? And the covenant described in verse 13 is even more perplexing, a covenant of priesthood. As the grandson of Aaron the first priest, Pinchas already was a member of the priestly class, as would be his direct male descendants for all eternity. So why does God give him a covenant he already is a part of? If we go back to the proscribed punishment and the precise language as stated by Rashi, *pogi'in* could mean kill, but it also can mean approach or confront. Moses had commanded the Judges to kill the offenders, but Pinchas, a priest, jumps into the fray and assumes the role of judge, jury and executioner and in this process kills both Zimri and Cozbi even though the punishment cited by Rashi specifically says *bo*, him.

Now let us analyze the story from a new perspective. Pinchas is the grandson of Aaron, known according to our tradition as one who loved peace and pursued peace. Pinchas is a member of the priestly class, whose role and functions are to enable and effectuate the various *korbanot,* the offerings brought by the people or brought by the priests on behalf of the expiation of guilt for the people. He sees a situation of grave danger with serious implications for the Jewish people. He is aware of God's wrath and of Moses' command to the Judges. But his passion, his zealotry and perhaps his jealousy of the judges who have been called upon to enact God's word, consumes Pinchas. Rather than approach and confront Zimri with the seriousness of his crime, Pinchas takes a devastating leap of lack-of-faith in the process as laid out by Moses. He enacts what he believes is the absolute truth of God's wish, for Zimri and Cozbi to be killed, and in this process assumes several roles to which he had not been appointed. Perhaps this was the state of internal strife that led Pinchas to this violent action. For this he was bound by God into a covenant of peace, one that would enable him to relearn the message and mission of his grandfather Aaron, one in which first and foremost you attempt to peacefully resolve all situations. And because he had veered so far from the path of his grandfather Aaron, even in the midst of the thirty days of mourning, when Aaron's attributes should have been fresh in his eyes as Aaron's grandson, he and his descendants forever needed once again to be bound by God in a covenant of priesthood. And as priests, they would forever be required to understand that their role in serving the people and God, requires them to feel a weighty responsibility. While we are all responsible for the consequences of our actions, the priests must also bear the weighty responsibility they assume on behalf of the entirety of the Jewish people.

A passage that is part of the *Chazzan's* (cantor's) traditional prayer before *Mussaf* (the additional service) for both days of *Rosh Hashanah* (New Year) and Yom Kippur (Day of Atonement) states ". . . and may truth and peace co-exist." Rabbi Joseph B. Soloveitchik noted that:

> Absolute truth and absolute peace cannot coexist today,
> because insistence on absolute truth precludes peaceful

coexistence," and leaves it for messianic times for God to facilitate these two traits co-existing.[1]

Zealous pursuit of enforcing an Absolute Truth that we are so certain is reflective of God's will often finds us overstepping our roles, overreacting and acting harshly. And the consequences may be irreparable, not only to the victims of our actions but perhaps also to our selves.

1. Lustiger & Tauber, *Yom Kippur Machzor*, p.513.

SECTION V

JOURNEYS: THE PROCESS IS THE PRODUCT

20

"I PUT BEFORE YOU TODAY A BLESSING AND A CURSE"

THERE MAY A SIMPLE reason why many of us prefer to see things in black and white All puns intended, it is clearer and distinct, and in some ways for many, comforting to know, or to believe that we know, exactly what we are looking at. The Torah portion *Reah*, which ironically means "See," starts off with what appears to be a fairly black and white statement:

> See: I'm putting in front of you today a blessing and a curse. The blessing when you listen to the commandments of God, your God, that I commanded you today. And the curse if you don't listen the commandments of God, your God, and you will turn from the way that I commanded you today, to go after other gods, whom you haven't known. (Deut 11:26–28)

It is important to note that within these sentences there is a shifting in the Hebrew from the singular to the plural. Specifically the opening word "See" is expressed in the verb form of a command to an individual, yet all subsequent references to "your God," "commanded you," "you will turn" and "whom you haven't known" are in the plural form. So we must ask ourselves four questions. First, is God speaking to each of us as an individual or is this a communal statement, and if the latter, what does it mean for a community to be commanded to see something? Second, we have to wonder whether we think that experiential reality supports the idea that there is some type of blessing "before us" if we follow God's commandments and there is some type of curse if we don't. Third, do we merit this curse if we just don't follow God's commandments or do we also have to "go after other gods whom you haven't known" as well. And finally, did God just place before us this blessing and curse on that "today" in which this was stated, or is there a constant daily presentation of this choice option?

In order to answer these questions, we need to explore passages in a later section of the Torah portion, where we are cautioned against following false dreamers or prophets who produce signs or wonders as proof that we should follow other gods "whom we haven't known." Throughout these verses, we also find a shifting back and forth from the singular to the plural, as was the case in the opening lines.

> When a prophet or one who has a dream will get up among you [singular] . . .and the sign or the wonder of which he spoke to you [singular] saying, Let us [plural] go after other gods whom you [plural] haven't known and serve them. You [singular] shall not listen to that prophet's words . . . because your [plural] God is testing you [plural] to know whether you [plural] are loving God . . . And the prophet or that one who has the dream shall be put to death . . . So you [singular] shall burn away what is bad from among you [singular]. (Deut 13:2–6)

God has given us a gift, an eternal and forever renewing gift, of revelation. The reference in the opening lines to "today" is not meant to that specific day on which the words were stated or for that matter to that day when the penultimate revelation occurred at Mt. Sinai. "Today" or *hayom* in Hebrew, teaches us two things. According to the Midrash Tanchuma (Deut 26:16) the Torah should be always as dear to us as it was on that day, on that *hayom*, when we received it at Mt. Sinai. And Rashi's interpretation of the very same word in that verse is that we are obliged to see within the Torah new things or ideas every day.

But the idea of a daily revelation with the concomitant opportunity for daily renewal is a double-edged sword. We have the capacity to create for ourselves, both in the singular and in the plural, as individuals and as a people, ideas and thoughts that may serve as blessings or curses for us. Having experienced, in the collective historical sense and perhaps even in some Jungian-like collective unconscious sense, a taste of the Divine and the transcendent at Mt. Sinai, we are open to the visions of the dreamer or the prophet. Because there is much that is by definition inexplicable, we are challenged and commanded both as individuals and as a community to struggle with and discover and rediscover anew, and as new, the voice and vision of God in our lives. But this makes us vulnerable to "false voices." These voices may be external to us, but also may reside deep within ourselves. God's "testing" of us is not some simplistic game of black and white obedience with a neatly defined product. The daily test is one of process. How do we as individuals and as a community struggle to understand the mysteries of the un-understandable? Our love of God, or the lack of thereof, isn't neatly demonstrated by blind obedience to commandments, but rather by how we struggle with this challenge. It is based on whether we participate in the process of a constant, daily-and-forever struggle to find and connect to God, even though we may fear the possibilities of false dreamers or prophets from within or from without. The evil of the dreamer or the prophet that we are commanded to eradicate from our midst is not their vision. We are warned against being swayed by their attempt to turn us away from the process of the struggle by offering us as a simplistic vision. This vision is falsely garbed in signs and wonders that are illusions of certainty and truth, a vision of a god who is not our God, the God we have known at Sinai.

What awaits us each *hayom*, each day, is an opportunity that we can seize and turn into a blessing for ourselves. Or we can avoid the opportunity out of rigidity, complacency or fear, which ultimately will be a curse for us. There may not be a simple, constant, never-changing vision, and we may not always see things the same way every day, whether as an individual or as a community. But we are nonetheless commanded to take that daily leap of faith, to "See!"

21

WHY WE NEED RAILINGS AROUND THE ROOFS OF OUR HOUSES

ONE OF THE FASCINATING, seemingly practical commandments we have in the book of Deuteronomy is the requirement to put a railing on the roof of a new house we build. At first blush from a reading of the text, this appears to be fairly straightforward:

> When you'll build a new house, you shall make a railing for your roof, so you won't set blood upon your house when someone will fall from it. (Deut 22:8)

In the rabbinic accounting of the commandments contained in this verse, found in some classic Hebrew editions of the Torah such as the *Mikraot Gedolot*,[1] this sentence is comprised of two commandments, one a positive commandment and the other a negative commandment. The positive commandment is to construct our homes in accordance with standards that will minimize danger and to remove all obstacles and dangers from all our dwelling places. The negative commandant is that we are forbidden to place or create any obstacles or endangering situations in our land and in our houses.

---

1. Berman, Z. *Mikraot Gedolot*, Vol.5, p. 245.

But our text is fascinating because it is not worded as broadly as the above seems to imply. In fact several questions emerge. If safety is the issue, the wording in the Torah should not be limited to building a new house. Our culpability and therefore responsibility should apply to anything that we own, whether we build it as a new dwelling or buy an older, previously built home. And if general safety is the concern, why is the specific detail mentioned here about a railing on the roof of the structure? Why not window guards, or for that matter anything else that could enhance our safety around a potential environmental hazard? And why don't we forbid someone from going up to the roof completely so that they are never placed in a situation of potential danger? The Torah's language regarding the victim of a non-railed roof is also interesting, in that we are not told " . . .lest someone go up to your roof and fall . . ." as the translation of the sentence is shown above. Rather, a closer translation of the Hebrew text is " . . .because when the falling one will fall . . ." Why is this person already dubbed "the falling one?" And lastly, a type of question often asked by classical biblical commentators, what is the significance of this commandment's placement immediately following the verse that tells us the requirement of sending away a mother bird before we remove her eggs from her nest, a mitzvah that is symbolic of the high value placed on compassion as a required attribute for a Jew?

The two simplest ways to fall off the roof of a house that is non-railed is if you get too close to the edge while you've either got your head focused up in the clouds or while you're focused on looking down on what's below. The "new house" can possibly symbolize the constructs that we as human beings create, which, if unguarded, we can allow to go to our head, our "roofs." Maybe we are convinced that our ideas are so noble or so right that we've got our head up in the clouds, assuming that we've unraveled the mysteries of the universe and God. Or perhaps we're focused on looking down on those whose views differ from us. Either way, we are destined and doomed to fall. And the culpability rests with us because we have opportunities to create personal safeguards against these ways of thinking, however appealing and tempting they may be. We, like the person who falls off the roof in the text, make the decision to go up to the roof in the first place without the necessary precautions.

And what are those precautions? A rail or a fence. While our text uses an unusual Hebrew word, *maakeh*, for fence, there are two famous statements of the Talmudic rabbis that advise us to create important fences, both cited in Mishna Avot. The first is " . . .make a fence round the Torah." (Avot 1:1). And later it says ". . .a fence to wisdom is silence." (Avot 3:20). We all seek to protect our views and beliefs that we hold dear and believe to be true. The question is do we need to create a fence to protect our traditions from some external threat, or to protect them from the dangers and dangerous situations we create ourselves, which can potentially threaten our tradition? Do we put up fences that serve as barriers to understanding our traditions fully or inhibit our ability to access other perspectives? What are the positive ways in which we might not impulsively respond to others whose views on Jewish tradition differ from our own? Can we understand that differing views needn't be resolved via an argument in which one is found to be "truer" than the other? And perhaps most importantly, can we understand that there is great wisdom in a silence in which you are truly able to listen, to fully attend to and consider the other person's views?

And finally, we have a lesson of compassion. As Jews, we are called upon to be sensitive to the ways in which we could hurt or injure the "feelings" of a mother bird when we take her eggs away. We are in effect commanded to pause and understand the pain we are about to inflict on another of God's living creatures. How much more so must we be cognizant of what we could do to other human beings when we look down upon them from our illusory "ivory" towers of our own creation.

22

SHABBAT HAAZINU AND THE 7ᵀᴴ DAY OF PASSOVER
PARALLEL CAUTIONARY TALES

WE ARE TAUGHT BY our sages that we should experience the revelation at Mount Sinai anew every day (Rashi on Deut 11:13). One of the ways in which we serendipitously fulfill this is when we have an epiphany, an experience of reading some Jewish canonical text and suddenly, remarkably feel as if we have never before seen it, much less understood it or its religious meaning for us. Recently, on the *Shabbat* of *Haazinu* following Yom Kippur, I realized for the first time that the *haftorah* (prophetic portion) read that morning is the very same portion from Samuel II that is also read on the 7th day of Passover. That was my epiphany experience. But then the challenge before me was to understand what, if any, was the parallel between the 7th day of Passover and the *Shabbat* that immediately follows Yom Kippur.

The Torah portion we read on the 7th day of Passover recounts the exodus from Egypt, but particularly the story of God enabling the Jewish people to cross through the Red Sea while the Egyptians drowned in pursuit of them. The famed "*Shirat Ha Yam*" (the Song of the Sea), which Moses sings, acknowledges the peril, persecution and the deliverance that each individual Jew and our people as a whole felt. And the result of this experience was such that, as we read right before the song " . . .and they believed in God and Moses his servant." (Exod 14:31) In looking at the *haftorah* for the 7th day of Passover, Rabbi Joseph Hertz refers to it as a " . . .magnificent Song of Thanksgiving . . .David . . .traces Divine Providence in his own marvelous escapes from persecution and peril, and renders thanks to God Almighty for his deliverance and victories."[1] It is therefore very easy to see the wisdom in the selection of the *haftorah* to parallel the Torah portion for the 7th day of Passover.

In assigning this very same haftorah to the Shabbat of *Haazinu* when Moses speaks to the Jewish people prior to his death, one could easily argue that the parallel is also about the deliverance through the perils and persecution of the journey through the desert prior to the impending entry into Israel. But what is the particular meaning of this *haftorah* within the context of the Torah portion of *Haazinu* being read on the Shabbat that comes immediately after Yom Kippur? In a very simple, almost basic level, if we survive Yom Kippur and are blessed to be in synagogues, to hear the reading of *Haazinu*, then it is cause for a song of thanksgiving that we as individuals and as a collected assembly would want to sing, thanking God for delivering us from our perils. But perhaps there is an even more profound and cautionary parallel that should give us cause for reflection. In Exodus, our redemption at the Red Sea was part of a two-fold miracle that we experienced, culminating weeks later with the revelation of God and the Torah at Mount Sinai. Various rabbinic stories recount the incredible miracles that occurred and the level of holiness and prophecy that even the most "common" of Jews experienced at Sinai.[2] And yet, two weeks later, we as a people participate in the creation of the Golden Calf, sinking to an inexplicable low moral level. And what is the parallel that follows our apparent redemption and salvation of living to experience the Shabbat of *Haazinu* following Yom Kippur? It is the holiday of *Succot*, Tabernacles, where we live in booths and attempt to connect

1. Hertz, J., p. 904.

2. See earlier reference to [even] a maidservant having a high level of holiness and prophecy as the result of the revelation experience.

to the incredible fragility and vulnerability, both physically and spiritually, which reflects the true reality of our lives.

The reading of the same *haftorah* on these two days comes to alert us to several things. First, we must always understand the ultimate source of our redemption and salvation and give appropriate thanks to God. But perhaps even more importantly, we cannot ever assume that that we have been completely redeemed or saved. We journeyed from the Red Sea to Mount Sinai to the Golden Calf and then forty years in the desert, during which time nearly the entire generation that had left Egypt died. Similarly, we journey from the awe and trepidation of Yom Kippur to the life-affirming Shabbat following, but then are thrust immediately into our fragile and vulnerable booths for the holiday of Succot. This is the cycle of Jewish life and it is the cycle of all of our personal lives. We are always in the process of becoming, searching and journeying. Our task is to take part in the journey to our best effort. We are ever-changing and hopefully improving, but always being cautious about declarations of having arrived, much less being certain of our redemption or salvation.

23

WHY WE CAN NEVER KNOW MOSES' BURIAL PLACE

IN THE CONCLUDING CHAPTER of Deuteronomy, we end the five books of the Torah with the description of Moses' death.

> And Moses, God's servant, died there in the land of Moab by God's mouth. And He buried him in the valley in the land of Moab opposite Beth Peor. And no man knows his burial place to this day. And a prophet did not rise again in Israel like Moses, whom God knew face-to-face ... (Deut 34:6–10)

Friedman, commenting on the opening line and the Hebrew *vayikbor,* "and He buried him" in the singular [referring to God], notes that there are alternative traditions in Qumran, Septuagint and some manuscripts of the Samaritan tradition that have the Hebrew word with an additional *vav* at the end, transforming this to *vayikbiru,* "and they buried him."[1] The differences inherent in the variant texts are extraordinary in our conceptualization of Moses' death scene. In the first, Moses is alone on top of Mount Nebo. He is shown the land promised to Abraham, Isaac and Jacob that he will not enter, and God then facilitates his death, and God then buries Moses. In the latter alternative manuscripts, Moses must have come down from the mountain to some lower point, as

1. Friedman, ibid, p. 678.

Friedman describes, and dies there, perhaps surrounded by other people, and then they bury him. Two very different scenes, with different messages for us. Friedman suggests the traditional text has Moses dying alone in contradistinction to the other manuscripts' variant text where he is among his fellow human beings. One could equally argue that for anyone, and perhaps particularly for Moses, dying with just [sic] God is anything but alone and in fact could represent a profoundly spiritual experience for Moses. Moreover, given what we know from the Torah about Moses in general, his Revelation experience, the need to at times wear a veil and the verse that " . . .a prophet did not rise again in Israel like Moses" it isn't clear that Moses really had "fellow human beings" in a social sense as we understand it.

Let's focus on Moses' burial place. While not quite the same as the results we're now used to when doing a directions search on Google Maps, nonetheless we are give some specifics about where Moses is buried. But this begs the question, Why tell us any details regarding the location if we are destined never to know his burial place? Our text reads like a tantalizing clue, tempting us to do exactly what we might think is the direct opposite of what God appears to be trying to achieve. That is, the description simply whets the appetite and fuels the adventurous spirit of treasure seekers and others who would want to find Moses' burial place. Why is God tempting us, and perhaps more importantly, why are we never to know Moses' burial place? There is no other such prohibition regarding the burial place of any other figure in the Torah. Certainly from a pragmatic standpoint, we know that the purported burial places of the patriarchs and the matriarchs and Rachel's Tomb are venerated spots to which access is encouraged.

We do, however, have one model for protecting a place to which God does not want people to go. After being banished from the Garden of Eden, God places cherubs and a flaming sword to the east of the Garden to prevent access to it and to the Tree of Life (Gen. 3:24.). So why didn't God simply place similar cherubs and a flaming sword by Moses' burial place?

While the idea of God placing cherubs, or even fire, to guard access to Moses' burial place might have been a neat literary device, an analysis of the difference of the two desired outcomes may shed some light for us. The banishment of Adam and Eve and the protection of the Tree of Life represent the message that we, humanity, cannot and should not return to the idyllic life symbolized by the Garden. We were given a new destiny, one in which we would forever struggle but have the capacity to create, recreate, and benefit from the fruits of our labor. Access back into the Garden is what is denied us, but "knowing" it or seeing it is not, for it could even serve as a reminder of our new role and responsibility in the world.

Interestingly, for all our veneration of Moses, for all that he is forever to be called *Moshe Rabbeinu*, Moses, our teacher, there will never be, there can never be another human like him. Knowledge of his burial place could lead to an idolization that would in effect create another "god." Moses would have become an untenable standard against which we would all fall far from the mark. God selected Moses and gave him a mission and Moses evolved over time and became a great prophet and leader. That was his mission and there will never be another person selected with that unique mission. Moses succeeded in fulfilling his mission, although far from perfect. He faithfully made the long journey and our text rather uniquely defines him as one " . . .whom God knew face-to-face." That is, God was blessed [as it were] to see Moses achieve the full realization of his potential.

A classic Chassidic story, told by many, is about the famed eighteenth-century Chassidic Rabbi, Zusha of Anipoli. On his deathbed, tears were streaming down his eyes. His students were dismayed and asked why he was crying. He replied that when he died and came before the Heavenly tribunal, he was not afraid that God would ask him why he wasn't like Moses, but rather that God would ask him why he wasn't like Reb Zusha, why he hadn't realized his inner potential, and for this he would have no answer.

Each of us is created as a completely unique individual and it is our life-long journey and struggle to discover what our mission might be and how we can best go about pursuing that mission. We are not called upon to be Moses. God needs us to be the very best you or me that we can be. That is our mission, and we are not in competition to be anybody else, much less to be better than somebody else. If, like Moses, we succeed, then there will also never rise again someone like each of us, and we too will merit the blessing that God has seen us face-to-face.

AFTERWORD

EACH OF US CONTAINS within our souls some trace element of that primary revelatory experience at Sinai. Not a sharp, clear-focused vision, but a hazy, obscured, yet nonetheless phenomenal experience, to which we are bidden to reconnect with daily. We are all common partners in an individual and group journey through life to return to Sinai and perhaps to see what we can discover anew about it and ourselves. In order to achieve this goal, we would need to be open to the limitless possibilities and insights that can infuse our mind so we can awaken daily to a new revelation and a new experience of the revelation. All this can serve as a great equalizer, a common core element that can move us to look at each other with recognition, respect, and humility.

Unfortunately, we find ourselves as citizens of the world confronting daily examples of strife and dissent. At its "best," contentious disagreements paralyze elected officials and whole countries from taking the necessary steps to better the lives of their citizens. Lines are drawn in the sand between religions, believers and non-believers, people of differing political opinions, etc. At its worst, we have war, terrorism and acts of violence in which no one is spared from the horrors and no end or "good" end is in sight.

Focusing solely on our internal struggles, the global Jewish community is not immune to these problems and is often characterized by intense internecine feuding. Across all denominational affiliations, we often speak with absolute certainty of "Truth" and the truths we claim to possess. This theological arrogance results in fixed unyielding pronouncements of what God wants and doesn't want, of what processes God favors and doesn't favor, of what one group knows to be True and another group knows with equal dogmatic certainty is not True, who is defending Judaism and who is contributing to its demise, and countless other statements of extreme polarity and hostility. Where is the dynamic sense of the process that should shed new light daily, widely attributed to the Kotzker Rebbe " . . .if one's concept of God today is exactly as it was yesterday, it is tantamount to worshipping idols." The inherent and often thinly veiled triumphalism expressed by each group, certain that they are the true inheritor and transmitter of the Sinaitic experience, is astonishing. Yes, there is room for passion and commitment, which can appropriately lead to differing beliefs and practices, as well as concerns and fears about what is right for the Jews and the Jewish people. But competition for the uncontested title of "Defender of the Truth" and "Champion of What God Really Wants and/or Doesn't Want a Jewish Person to Be/Do/ Say/Think/Feel/Believe/Pray" is fierce, and there are no shortage of self-proclaimed champions. This is a far cry from a notion of truly experiencing revelation and God anew on a daily basis. With this competitive mindset, we are unable to wake up each morning with a wondrous excitement based on doubt and uncertainty that are not foibles, but rather necessary strengths. The theological arrogance we see and hear belies delusions of grandeur, in which we have refashioned ourselves, not in the image of God, but as mini Gods; or even worse, as God's attorneys and marketing reps who do all the talking for their client. We become guilty of exactly that which the Rabbis in the Talmud (*Sotah*, 5a) warned us against " . . . any person who possesses haughtiness of spirit, the Holy One, blessed be He, declares, 'I and he cannot both dwell in the world.'"

The challenge we face daily is that, like our patriarch Jacob, we are all hobblers along a path, with obscured and limited vision, struggling between two polar extremes. At one extreme, we can simply miss God's presence in the world. This can manifest itself in a lack of appreciation or lack of recognition of God's role in the holy and the mundane, the extraordinary and the ordinary. It can take on larger proportions, as our "I," whether as an individual, group, cohort, school of thought or denomination, becomes so large that it displaces and replaces God's presence. And at the other extreme, it may be expressed in our certainty that our experience of and relationship to God gives us the sole ability to know God and God's Truth, to the exclusion of others. Rather than recognizing that as human beings we are forever limited in our ability to know God, we remain Jacob's children, attempting to assert control and domination over that which we can never really possess.

When the prophet Isaiah uttered the famed words, "And the earth will be filled with the knowledge of God as the ocean covers the sea-bed," (Isaiah 11:9) he expressed a vision of a future, messianic time when knowledge of God might be possible. And even in this vision of the ideal, it is the earth, and not people, that will in some way be filled with the knowledge of God. Whether we as human beings will be able to have knowledge of God in messianic times is not clear. Perhaps we will still remain challenged and limited in our ability to attain that level of closeness and awareness. Zornberg, commenting upon the book of Exodus as a book of revelation, notes that " . . . the motif of 'not knowing' pervades the book, indeed, the whole Torah . . . the consciousness persists of a 'cloud of unknowing:' of another world, perhaps adjacent to this one, partially intimated, not mastered."[1]

Daily we have a clarion call that challenges us to experience revelation anew. It is an opportunity to ask ourselves where we are, who we are, where we are going and who we can and want to be, and then to ask those same questions again the next day, while seeking different answers. We stand at the base of the smallest, most humble of mountains. While it is becoming morning and light, all is not clear; we are all enveloped in smoke and clouds. Despite our impulse to proclaim ourselves as having a better vantage point or greater clarity of vision, we are not Moses atop Mount Sinai. There is no contest. There is no race and there is no fight,

1. Zornberg, ibid. p.212.

but we are all called upon to be players. There are no winners, but potentially there are many losers if we don't seek new ways of relating to each other as Jews and as human beings.

Bibliography

Berman, Z. *Chumash Mikraot Gedolot*. Union City, NJ: Gross Bros., 1991.

Bialik, C. and Ravinitsky, Y. *Sefer HaAgadah (The Book of Legends)*. Tel Aviv, Israel: Dvir, 1948.

Dennis, G. *The Encyclopedia of Jewish Myth, Magic and Mysticism*. Woodbury, MD: Llewelyn, 2007.

Friedman, R.E. *Commentary on the Torah*. San Francisco: Harper San Francisco, 2003

Gevrayahu, G. and Sicherman,H. "What Never Was and Never Will be: Rebellious Son—Subverted City—Infected House." *Jewish Bible Quarterly* (2001) 29.4.

Hertz, J., ed. *The Pentateuch and the Haftorahs: Hebrew Text, English Translation and Commentary*. New York: Metzudah, 1941.

Heschel, A. J. *God in Search of Man*. New York: Farrar, Straus & Giroux, 1955

———. *Man's Quest for God: Studies in Prayer & Symbolism*. New York: Scribners, 1954.

———. *The Sabbath: Its Meaning for Modern Man*. New York: Noonday, 1951.

Hirsch, Samson Raphael. *The Psalms* (Translation and Commentary). New York: Philipp Feldheim, 1960.

Jacobs, Jill. "Midrash Rabbah: One Name, Many Books." My Jewish Learning. Online: www.MyJewishLearning.com.

Lorberbaum, Y. "Two Concepts of Gezerat Ha-Katuv: A Chapter in Maimonides' Legal and Halakhic Thought; Part II: The Jurisprudential Sense." In *Evidence in Jewish Law*, edited by S. Ettinger, 101–37. Jerusalem: Institute for Legislative Research, 2011.

Lustiger, A. and Tauber, M. *Yom Kippur Machzor, with Commentary Adapted from the Teachings of Rabbi Joseph B. Soloveitchik*. New York: K'hal, 2006.

Maimonides, M. *Mishneh Torah*. www.sefaria.org, 2014.

Midrash, The. www.sefaria.org, 2014.

Sacks, J. "Covenant & Conversation," *Bamidbar*, May 24, 2014.

Saint Exupéry, A. *The Little Prince*. Translated by Richard Howard. New York: Harvest, 2000.

Schorsch, I. "Chancellor's Parashah Commentary, *Parashat Va-era*, Exodus 6:2-9:35." New York: Jewish Theological Seminary, January 24, 1998/26 Tevet 5758.

Siegel, S. "Imitatio Dei." In *Berenbaum*, edited by M & F. Skolnik, F. *The Encyclopedia Judaica* 2nd ed. Detroit: Macmillan, 2007.

Talmud, The Babylonian. www.sefaria.org, 2014

Zornberg, A. *The Particulars of Rapture: Reflections on Exodus.* New York: Doubleday, 2001